Anonymous

The Great Jennens Case

Being an epitome of the history of the Jennens family

Anonymous

The Great Jennens Case
Being an epitome of the history of the Jennens family

ISBN/EAN: 9783337328139

Printed in Europe, USA, Canada, Australia, Japan

Cover: Foto ©ninafisch / pixelio.de

More available books at **www.hansebooks.com**

THE GREAT JENNENS CASE:

BEING AN

EPITOME OF THE HISTORY

OF

THE JENNENS FAMILY.

COMPILED ON BEHALF OF THE JENNENS FAMILY

BY

MESSRS. HARRISON & WILLIS.

SHEFFIELD:
PRINTED BY PAWSON AND BRAILSFORD, HIGH STREET AND MULBERRY ST.
1879.

DUFFIELD CHURCH.

INDEX.

A.
	PAGES.
Ambrose, Jane	7
Andover, Lady	17, 19, 20, 115, 116, 122 to 126
Affidavits	34 to 36, 41, 42, 183 to 200
Administration de bonis non Robert Jennens	39
,, Roger Ganney	207, 208
,, Anne Jennens	208
Acton Place	80, 82 to 85, 99 to 101, 113, 114
Acton Church	101 to 105
Anecdotes of Wm. Jennens, of Acton	85 to 89, 98 to 101, 113, 114
,, Sir Harvey Elwes	93 to 98
Application for Marriage Licence	79, 80

B.
Beard, Ellen	4
Bible, Family	17, 56, 57, 137
Boucher's, Wm., Affidavit	34
Bridgeons, Dorothy	54
Blyth, John and Mary	55
Blyth, Thomas and Mary	55
Baylis, Samuel and Mary	55
Blyth, Ann	56
Blyth, Elizabeth	56
Biggs, Joseph and Mary	56
Baylis, Samuel and Charlotte	55
Baylis, James	55
Baylis, James, Affidavit of	200
Bell, Rev. Arthur, Martyrdom of	80, 81
Betham's Baronetage on the descent of William Jennens	113
Burdett, Elizabeth	127

C.
Certificates of Baptisms, Marriages and Burials	12 to 15
Claimants' Pedigree	18
Curzon, Richard William (Earl Howe), Pedigree of	21
Catholics, Persecution of	60, 80, 81
Correspondence between Isaac and Elizabeth Perry, Mary Hodgetts, and Joseph and Ann Perry	63 to 67
Correspondence between Ann Patrick and Lady Andover	67 to 72
Correspondence between Richard Howard and Ann Patrick	72 to 76
Church, Acton	101 to 105

D.
	PAGES.
Demolition of Acton Place	113, 114
Doubts as to the date of the death of Lady Andover	.. 115

E.
Events, Principal, from 1509 to 1660 affecting the Jennens family	.. 6, 7
Essex, James and Mary	.. 55
Elwes, Sir Harvey	93 to 98
Elliott, Joan	.. 4

F.
Fraud, Definition of	.. 40
Family Relics	.. 55
Fisher, Sir Clement	.. 122

G.
Guidott, Ann	.. 62
Ganney, Roger	207, 208

H.
Handy, John	.. 55
Hood v. Beauchamp	58 to 62
Harrison, John and Hannah	.. 62
Harrison, William..	.. 9, 62
Hinch, Ann	.. 63
Harrison, Thomas	10, 62

I.
Identity of Mary Jennens' handwriting by Robert and Ann Jennens	38, 39

J.
Jennens Family, Supposed origin of	.. 3
Jennens, Robert (1545)	.. 4
Jennens, William (Mobourne Mill)	4, 22, 23
Jennens, various modes of spelling	15, 122
Jennens, Joan	23 to 28
Jennens, John (No. 1)	29 to 32, 141 to 152
Jennens, Mary (Cousin and Wife of John Jennens No. 1) ..	4
Jennens, Mary (Daughter of Humphrey Jennens) ..	38, 128, 129
Jennens, Robert, the elder ?..	37, 62, 78, 79
Jennens, Robert, the younger..	39, 62, 79, 90, 91, 92, 133 to 136
Jennens, Elizabeth	58, 119, 130
Jennens, John (No. 2)	53, 76, 77, 78
Jennens, John (No. 3)	.. 53

	PAGES.
Jennens, Roger	.. 9, 62
Jennens, Jacob and Ellen	.. 9, 62
Jennens, William, of Duffield	.. 9, 62
Jennens, Jacob and Betty	.. 9, 62
Jennens, Anne	.. 91
Jennens' Monument	103 to 107
Jennens, William, of Acton, Funeral of	.. 107
Jennens, William, Immense wealth of	107, 108
Jennens, Humphrey, the elder	117, 153 to 183
Jennens, Ann (Daughter of Humphrey Jennens)	117, 122, 208
Jennens, Esther	.. 117
Jennens, Charles	117, 127
Jennens, Ambrose	122, 208, 223
Jennens, Robert (Son of Humphrey Jennens)	130 to 133
Jennens, Hannah	.. 9, 62
Jennens, Martha	.. 9, 62
Jennens v. Norton	44 to 51
Johnson, William, Affidavit of	183, 184

L

Lygon, William	17, 19, 20
Licence, Marriage, Application for	79, 80
Letters of Administration, Robert Jennens	39, 90, 91, 92
,, Roger Ganney	207, 208
,, Anne Jennens	.. 208
,, Anne Jennens	.. 91

M

Mobourne Mill	.. 4, 5
Monk's, General, Letter to John Jennens (No. 3)	53, 54
Mellor, Ellen	.. 9, 62
Monument, The Jennens	103 to 107
Moore, Francis Wellington, Affidavit of	187, 188

N

Norton, Roger v. John Jennens	43 to 51

O

Obituary Notices of William Jennens, of Acton	107 to 112
,, ,, Lady Andover	115, 116

P

Pedigree of Claimants	.. 18
,, Present Owners	20, 21
Patrick, Thomas and Ann	.. 56
Patrick, Joseph and Mary	.. 184

iv

	PAGES.
Patrick, Mary (Sister-in-law to Ann Patrick), Affidavit of	184, 185
Perry, Isaac and Elizabeth	.. 56
Persecution of Catholics	60, 80, 81
Property, Personal, of William Jennens, of Acton	.. 108
Perren, John Brooke, Affidavit of	185 to 187

R

Randolph's, C. Leverson, Certificate and Affidavit	34 to 36
Rhodes, William and Eliza	.. 56
Rotherham, Isabel	.. 9, 62
Rhodes, Eliza, Affidavit of	188 to 192
Rhodes, Abraham Ward ⎫ Rhodes, Mary Ann ⎬ Joint Affidavit of Rhodes, William ⎬ Rhodes, Eliza ⎭	193 to 199

S

Somerton's, Elizabeth, Affidavit of	41, 42
Sherwood, Mary	.. 55
Saunders, Martha	.. 9, 62
Smith, Betty	.. 9, 62
Smith, Jeremiah and Elizabeth	38, 119

T

Truelock, Jane	.. 62
Temple, The Middle, Entry of Robert Jennens	.. 36

W.

Weaman, Joyce	.. 4
Whitehouse, Charlotte	.. 55
Willis, Daniel and Martha	10, 62
Willis, Thomas and Ruth	.. 62
Willis, George and Ann	62, 63
Worrall, Ruth	.. 63
Willis, Daniel (the younger) and Ann	.. 15
Will of William Jennens of Mobourne Mill and Birmingham	22, 23
,, Joan Jennens	23 to 28
,, William Jennens, of Acton	89, 90
,, Humphrey Jennens the elder	117 to 121, 153 to 183
,, Ambrose Jennens	122, 208 to 223
,, John Jennens (No. 1)	29 to 32, 141 to 152
,, Mary Howard (Lady Andover)	201 to 207
,, Mary Jennens	128, 129
,, John Jennens (No. 3)	200, 201

		PAGE
	Church and Mob....ll	7.
	St. Martin's Church, Birmingham	23
4.	Interior ditto ditto	29
5.	Town House of John Jennens (No. 1), Birmingham, 1653	44
6.	Acton Place	80
7.	Acton Place (another view)	100
8.	Acton Monument (Robert Jennens')	104
9.	Gopsal Hall	111
10.	Gopsal Chapel	112
11.	Erdington Hall	120
12.	Aston Hall	144
13.	Gopsal Church	222

WILLIAM JENNENS, DECEASED.

William Jennings, or Jennens, of Acton Place, near Long Melford, in the County of Suffolk, died at Acton Place on the 19th June, 1798, in the 98th year of his age. The history of this man is involved in mystery. Doubts have been entertained as to his parentage and also as to his assumed right to what have been long known as "The Jennings' estates." At his death he was deemed to have been the richest commoner in the United Kingdom, and as he died a bachelor and intestate, the event excited extraordinary interest. Considerable sums of money, amounting in the aggregate to nearly £100,000, have been spent in making enquiries and searches, for copies of documents and in useless litigation in this now well known case. No sooner was William Jennens dead than a host of claimants appeared, each one having his or her theory of descent from the paternal line, and each being supplied with certificates in proof. Some of the theories are startling and amusing, others appear to be too vague and remote, and hitherto all of them have failed to prove the pedigree. Without doubt many thousands of pounds have been honestly spent in the sincere belief of the justice of the claim; but it is to be feared that in too many instances large sums of money have been thrown away upon pretentious genealogists and others who, so long as they were paid their charges, were indifferent to the result. Many have been deceived and disappointed by their eagerness to adopt a certificate, whether of baptism, marriage or burial, wherever they found it "to fit in," little thinking at the time that identity must be established. There have been at least seventeen cases before the court :—three distinct claims by the Martin family, four distinct claims by Joseph Jennings family, five distinct claims by Elizabeth Jennings family, two distinct claims by Henry Jennens family, and three distinct claims by Edward Jennings family. It is said that it was from these vexations and long-pending suits that the late Charles Dickens derived the idea of "Jarndyce v. Jarndyce" in the popular novel of "Bleak House." After so many failures, one would think the case as almost hopeless. But no; there are other claimants in the field, who have reason to believe they will ultimately succeed. From discoveries recently made they are encouraged to hope; and they believe they will not only be able to prove a fraud, but that the greater portion of the property of the late William Jennens is impressed with a trust. Inquiries are being prosecuted, and even at this stage of the proceedings there is a *primâ facie* case. It is now intended to have carefully perused the vast mass of documentary evidence, and by a pedigree of clear and certain descent, and other evidence from various sources, to frame such a case as to satisfy any honest mind. Should the claim be satisfactorily established, there is little doubt as to success.

The particulars are dry in detail and will not interest an ordinary reader, but to the various members of the Jennens family they cannot fail to revive the hope of retributive justice. In giving the history of this remarkable case it will be necessary to quote from several books and documents which may be seen in the British Museum, the Parliament Office, House of Lords, Somerset House, and various provincial registries—notably those at Birmingham, Duffield, Lichfield and Salisbury. It is alleged that since the death of William Jennens in 1798, many fraudulent acts have been committed by interested parties, and numerous registers have been falsified, defaced and destroyed. If such be the case, the motive is obvious. Notwithstanding such unfair acts, a clue has been found, which is now being followed up, and the truth will be made manifest to the unbiassed reader.

After these few prefatory remarks, the following extracts from a manuscript in the British Museum as to the origin of the Jennings family will perhaps interest the reader:—

"The family of the Jennings is of very ancient origin. They seem to have been settled in England before the Norman conquest. They were of Danish extraction, and the first who settled in this kingdom appears to have been a Danish captain, brought into England by Canute, King of Denmark. Here he was baptised into the Christian faith, and had certain manors lying upon the sea coast near Harwich given him by Canute, as a reward for his former services done for his father, Sweyne, King of Denmark."

Little more is known of the family until the reign of Henry VIII., when one Robert Jennens is found employed in the royal household.

It appears that this Robert Jennens became a favourite of the king, who in or about 1545 promoted him, and after presenting him with a sword and belt (which it is said are still preserved), sent him to Shottle, in the parish of Duffield, in the county of Derby, to act there as chief warden deerstalker and ranger. Robert Jennens was married to one Ellen Beard, and had issue a son named William, who went to Birmingham, and married one Joanna Elliott, and had issue a son named John, who became a great ironmaster in Birmingham. This John was twice married —the first time to a cousin of his, Mary Jennens; the second time to one Joyce Weaman, the daughter of a wealthy solicitor at Birmingham. Having premised that Robert Jennens, of Shottle, was the father of William Jennens, of Shottle and of Birmingham (who died in 1602), and that the said William Jennens was the father of John Jennens, of Birmingham (who was twice married, and died in 1653), it will be comparatively easy to prove the remainder of the pedigree. In the above epitome only one child from each family has been selected, he being in the direct line of descent, thus: William, one of the sons of Robert; John, one of the sons of William. This will be seen on reference to the pedigree.

The above-named William Jennens purchased Mobourne Mill, at Duffield, and occasionally resided there. One of his sons, named William Jennens, appears to have died there in 1633, and in the register at Duffield he is described as of Mobourne Mill. His wife, Joanna Jennens, made two wills, copies of which are here given.

In these wills it will be seen that reference is made to a son John, and to a grandson John the son of John, so that the line of descent is as follows :—

1.—Robert Jennens, of Shottle, by Ellen, his wife.—*William*.

2.—William Jennens, of Birmingham, by Joanna, his wife.—*John*.

3.—John Jennens, of Birmingham, by Mary, his wife.—*John*.

Before proceeding further with the genealogy it will be now necessary to state a few facts incident to the case. It has been previously stated that many of the registers of baptisms, marriages, and burials have been wantonly injured by interested parties, and doubtless this is correct; but it is not suggested that all of them have been in the possession of the persons whose interest it was to destroy them. For instance, the register at Duffield commences in 1595, and the transcripts of same in the diocesan register at Lichfield commence in 1663. It is well known to every reader of English history that during the sieges of Lichfield, alternately by the Royal and Parliamentary forces, many valuable documents were lost. The beautiful cathedral was laid in ruins, and only a portion of the wills, inventories, and transcript registers were saved from destruction. This will account for the present defective state of the registers. Since 1595 and 1663 however, and particularly since 1798, there are instances of erasures and obliterations of entries relative to this case.

In perusing this narrative, it will be necessary to bear in mind the troublesome state of the times—to note the principal events that then occurred, and the dates, as affecting the movements of certain members of the Jennens family.

Henry VIII. reigned from 1509 to 1547, about which time Robert Jennens was sent to Shottle.

Edward VI. reigned from 1547 to 1553.

Mary reigned from 1553 to 1558.

Elizabeth reigned from 1558 to 1603.

James I. reigned from 1603 to 1625.

Robert Jennens died at Shottle in 1618.

William Jennens, of Mobourne Mill, the father of John (No. 1), died in 1602.

John (William's son) married his first wife in 1602.

Charles I. reigned from 1625 to 1649.

John (No. 2) married Jane Ambrose in 1636.

Charles I., in 1637, put his veto on emigration, and by a cruel fate detained his enemies.

In 1641, Charles I. intruded on the Commons, which caused the cry of "Privilege."

John (No. 2) suddenly left London in 1642.

In 1642 the civil war began.

In 1646 the suit Roger Norton *v.* John Jennens commenced.

DUFFIELD CHURCH.

MOBURN VILLA.

Robert Jennens (No. 1) born in 1644.
In 1649 Charles I. was beheaded.
John Jennens (No. 1) died in 1653.
Roger Jennings born 1653.
In 1653 Cromwell was declared Protector.
In 1658 Cromwell died.
John (No. 3) appointed Quarter-Master in Feb., 1659.
In 1660 Charles II. restored.
John (No. 3) married Dorothy Bridgeons in 1660.

He left his wife, and was absent from England 28 years.

It was during those momentous times that the Jennens family again acquired wealth and distinction,; but it is not unreasonable to suppose that, in common with many others, several members of the family by becoming partisans, became estranged to each other. The war was then raging throughout and desolating the country, and John Jennens (No. 2) had to retire from place to place to avoid its consequences. At one time he would be at Duffield (or rather at Mobourne Mill, which his father, John Jennens, of Birmingham, had given to him), at another time he would be either at London or Birmingham, but he appears to have been chiefly located at Reading, in the County of Berkshire, where in due time he attained the dignity of Mayor. This John Jennens appears to have married one Jane Ambrose (a distant relation by marriage), at East Garston Church, in Berkshire. The local register for 97 years prior to 1661, has been totally destroyed. To proceed now with the genealogy.

It has already been said that John Jennens (No. 1), of Birmingham, by his first wife Mary, had a son John (No. 2).

This latter John married Jane Ambrose, and had a son Roger, of whom mention will be made presently. The said John Jennens (No. 2) had also a son John (No. 3). This third John Jennings became a Quarter-Master in the Parliamentary Army, as appears by his appointment by General Monk.

If then John, the grandson of John (No. 1), took so active a part, it may be assumed there would be a conflict of feeling in the family, and this appears to have been the case from the tenor of John's (No. 1) will.

Now the will of John Jennens, of Birmingham, is dated the 25th day of February, 1651. It was prepared by his second wife's father, William Weaman, and the object of the will appears to have been to secure to the children of the second marriage with Joyce Weaman, the bulk of his real and personal estate. This animus is apparent throughout the will. Very little indeed appears to have been left by testator to the children of the first marriage. In justice, however, to testator, it must be observed that by making a deed of gift of Mobourne Mill to his son John, he may have sufficiently advanced him in life; but to this he does not allude in his will. He mentions his grandson John, whom he describes as the son of his *late* son John. The word "late," for some time past, raised a grave and apparently insuperable difficulty; but when it is remembered that by reason of the discord then prevalent,—the false rumours of accidents and of deaths incident to war—the active part afterwards taken by John (No. 3) under General Monk—the number of civilians as well as of military who were slain—the absence of a general post for the transmission of letters from one part of the country to another, it will not be surprising that doubts as to John's death may have been entertained. Whether the word "late" was honestly inserted by Mr. Weaman, the solicitor, in the belief of John's death will, perhaps, never be known, but certain it is, that testator's son John was then living, that he survived his father, and that he died at Mobourne Mill in 1673.

By this will, John Jennens devised his freeholds to his son Humphrey and his heirs; remainder to testator's son Joseph and his heirs; remainder to testator's son Edward and his heirs; remainder to testator's heirs on the body of Joyce Weaman; ultimate remainder to his own right heirs for ever. This penultimate remainder cannot in the least affect any after-acquired real estate owned by the family, or the personalty divisible amongst the next of kin of the intestate. Roger Jennens (the son of John Jennens No. 2, and the grandson of John Jennens No. 1) married Isabel Rotherham, by whom he had a son Jacob, who married Ellen Mellor, by whom he had a son William, who married Martha Saunders, by whom he had a son Jacob, who married Betty Smith, by whom he had two daughters, Hannah and Martha; Hannah Jennens was married to John Harrison, by whom she had two sons, William and

Thomas; Martha Jennens was married to Daniel Willis, by whom she had a daughter Ann and a son George.

The children therefore of Hannah Jennens and Martha Jennens, by their respective husbands John Harrison and Daniel Willis, claim to be descendants of Robert Jennens who was sent to Shottle by Henry VIII., in or about 1546, and who was the grandfather of John Jennens, of Birmingham, the great ironmaster, who died in 1653.

It has already been stated that John Jennens (No. 2) who married Jane Ambrose, had a son John (No. 3), whom it is necessary to mention, in consequence of certain of his descendants having claimed the estates. They claimed also to be entitled to a share of the personalty, as the representatives of the next of kin to the intestate. They failed to prove their case; in fact their case was never tried. Had they been then possessed of the proofs which have been recently obtained, the result might have been different; and should the descendants of Hannah Jennens and Martha Jennens succeed in establishing their title to the estates, or to any portion thereof, and derive any substantial advantage therefrom, it is their intention to recognise all their known relations, and to discover, as far as they practically can, all the lineal descendants of John Jennens of Birmingham, who died in 1653, with the view to the legal apportionment of the personal estate of the intestate (William Jennens, who died in 1798), in accor-

dance with the Statute of Distributions; for the persons who were legally entitled to share in the personalty of the late William Jennens, the intestate, were ignored by the administrator and administratrix, and as can be proved by the autograph letters of the late Lady Andover, and her son-in-law, Mr. Richard Howard, their relationship was disclaimed. It must be here observed that in a case of intestacy, the following relations are considered as and of the same degree of kindred:—
1st. Parents and children. 2nd. Grandfather, grandson and brother. 3rd. Great-grandfather, great-grandson, uncle and nephew. 4th. Great-great-grandfather, great-great-grandson, *great-uncle*, great-nephew, first cousin. The half-blood take equally with the whole blood in the same degree.

John Jennens (No. 2) who married Jane Ambrose, had, in fact, five children, namely,—Jane, John (No. 3), William, Robert and Roger. John (No. 3) and Roger have been already mentioned. The families or lines of Jane, William and Robert are extinct.

Robert Jennens, the third son of John (No. 2) and Jane Jennens, married Jane Truelock, by whom he had a son Robert, who married Anne Guidott, by whom he had a son William. This son, William Jennens, is the intestate, who died at Acton Place, in 1798. Consequently, Roger Jennens, who married Isabel Rotherham, was intestate's paternal great-uncle,—and it is seen that it is from Roger Jennens the present claimants trace their descent. If, then, the great-uncle and his legal representatives are entitled to a share of the personalty, in justice they should have it.

But some will say,—How can it be proved that the Shottle and the Birmingham families are identical, and even if that be, how can it be further proved that the intestate was the great-grandson of John Jennens (No. 2)? All this will be proved presently.

Assuming that the persons referred to in the certificates of baptisms, marriages and burials (which are mainly relied upon for establishing the requisite proofs) can be identified as members of the family of John Jennens (No. 1), then the line of descent will be reasonably traced. Failing such identification by reason of defective registers, such additional proofs—as family relics and traditions—will be submitted as evidence, and duly verified if necessary.

The following certificates of baptisms, marriages and burials have been obtained:—

The burial of Robert Jennens, of Shottle.

*The burial of William Jennens, of Birmingham.—Son.

†The burial of William Jennens, of Mobourne Mill.—Grandson.

†The burial of John Jennens, of Birmingham (No. 1).—Grandson.

‡The baptism of John Jennings, of Birmingham.—Great-grandson.

---

* Son of Robert.
† Sons of William, John (No. 1).
‡ John (No. 2).

An affidavit as to the marriage of John Jennens (No. 2) and Jane Ambrose.

The baptism of John (No. 3).

The baptism of Robert, son of John (No. 2), duly verified by the clergyman who gave it; since then the original entry has been erased from the register.

The baptism of Roger Jennens, son of John (No. 2); since this certificate was given the register has been tampered with.

The marriage of Robert Jennens to Jane Truelock.

The burial of Jane, the wife of John Jennens (No. 2).

The baptism of Robert, son of Robert and Jane Jennens.

The burial of John Jennens (No. 2).

The marriage of Roger Jennens to Isabel Rotherham.

The baptism of Jacob, the son of Roger and Isabel Jennens.

The marriage of Robert (son of Robert Jennens) to Anne Guidott.

The baptism of William Jennens (the intestate).

The burial of Roger Jennings.

The marriage of Jacob Jennings to Ellen Mellor.

The baptism of William, the son of Jacob Jennings.

The burial of Robert Jennens, of Bedford Row, at Acton.

The burial of Robert Jennings, of Bedford Row, at St. Andrew's, Holborn, London,

The burial of Ellen, the widow of Jacob Jennings.

The marriage of William Jenney and Martha Saunders.

The burial of Jacob Jennings.

The baptism of Jacob, son of William Jennings.

The burial of Anne, the widow of Robert Jennens.

The marriage of Jacob Jennings to Betty Smith.

The baptism of Hannah, daughter of Jacob and Betty Jenney.

The burial of William Jennings, great grandson of John (No. 2).

The marriage of John Harrison to Hannah Jenny.

The burial of William Jenny, of Shottle. The certificate is misdated 1703, instead of 1803. This William Jenny, or Jennings, survived William Jennings the intestate five years, and, it is submitted, he was entitled to certain real estate as heir-at-law, and also to a share of the personalty.

The baptism of William, son of John and Hannah Harrison.

The baptism of Thomas, son of John and Hannah Harrison.

The marriage of Daniel Willis to Martha Jennings.

The baptism of Thomas, son of Daniel and Martha Willis.

An entry in "The Pilgrim's Progress" of the birth of George, the son of Daniel and Martha Willis. It seems that George Willis was baptised at home, and the clergyman omitted to make an entry in the book. The book has been carefully preserved.

The baptism of Elizabeth, daughter of Daniel and Martha Willis.
The burial of Jacob Jennings, of Shottle.
The baptism of Sarah, daughter of Daniel and Martha Willis.
The baptism of Daniel, son of Daniel and Martha Willis.
The burial of Martha, wife of Daniel Willis.
The burial of Daniel Willis.

It will have been seen that the name of Jennens, or Jennings, has been variously spelt by different branches of the family, and the spelling usually represents the pronunciation of the name in the localities whence the certificates have been obtained. This, however, it is submitted, will not in any way interfere with the identity of the parties, for in those days, and even until very recently, spelling was simply reckless, and it will be observed, on referring to the office copies of wills and other documents herein referred to, that the word Jennens has been spelt in four different ways in one short will. Seldom, indeed, is it found to be the case that one mode of spelling has been adhered to.

This is mentioned to prevent any doubt as to the identity of any branch of the family claiming relationship to the intestate.

The name is sometimes spelt "Jennens," "Jenens," "Jenings," "Jennings," "Jenny," "Jenney," "Ganney" (soft G); &c., &c. Still the members claiming kindred have their traditions, heirlooms and pedigrees, which, if taken as a whole, prove they are descended from John Jennens, of Birmingham, who died in 1653.

Nearly all the registers containing entries of the baptisms, marriages and deaths of the descendants of John (No. 2) have been mutilated, falsified or destroyed.

It will have been seen that the late William Jennings, of Acton Place, who died in 1798 intestate, was the great-great-grandson of John Jennens, of Birmingham, who died in 1653.

Thus, John (No. 1), who died in 1653, had a son named John (No. 2), who died in 1673, leaving a son named Robert, who died in 1683, leaving a son named Robert, who died in 1725, leaving a son named William, who died in 1798 a bachelor and intestate.

The heir-at-law, then, must be sought for in the male line of John (No. 2). It will be remembered that John (No. 2) had four sons, namely:—John (No. 3), William, Robert and Roger. No one has as yet succeeded in court in tracing descent from John (No. 3). It is ascertained that the line of William, the second son, is extinct; and Robert's line became extinct on the death of William Jennens, the intestate. So that there only remain the descendants of Roger to make good their claim. It must be admitted that the case at this point is not without difficulty. The register at Duffield, which contained an entry of Roger's baptism, and of which a certificate was given, has since the date of the certificate been tampered with. Fortunately, however, the descendants of John Jennens (No. 2) have in their possession an old family Bible, which was presented by John (No. 1) to his son John (No. 2) on the occasion of his marriage with Jane Ambrose. In this Bible are duly recorded the births of all the children of John (No. 2). The names and dates agree with those in the local registers of baptisms, and have always been acknowledged by the members of the family as evidence of the pedigree.

The chief point in dispute is the paternity of William Jennens, the intestate. At the time of intestate's death certain other persons then living claimed to be descendants of John Jennens (No. 1) by his second marriage with Joyce Weaman:—namely, Mary Lady Andover, his great-granddaughter and granddaughter of Ann who had married Sir Clement Fisher, and William Lygon, his great-grandson. Utterly disclaiming all POOR relations, these two persons claimed to be the *only* next of kin to the intestate. There are grave doubts entertained as to the honesty of these two claims. But the said Lady Andover and William Lygon claimed that intestate was their cousin-german once removed, and alleged that he was the son of Robert, who was one of the sons of Humphrey Jennens. A reference to the sketch of the two pedigrees hereinafter given will explain the respective grounds of claim, and it will be better before entering upon the proofs of the identity of each of the said

c

Roberts to give the line of each descent, the claimants' pedigree being shown surrounded by a black line.

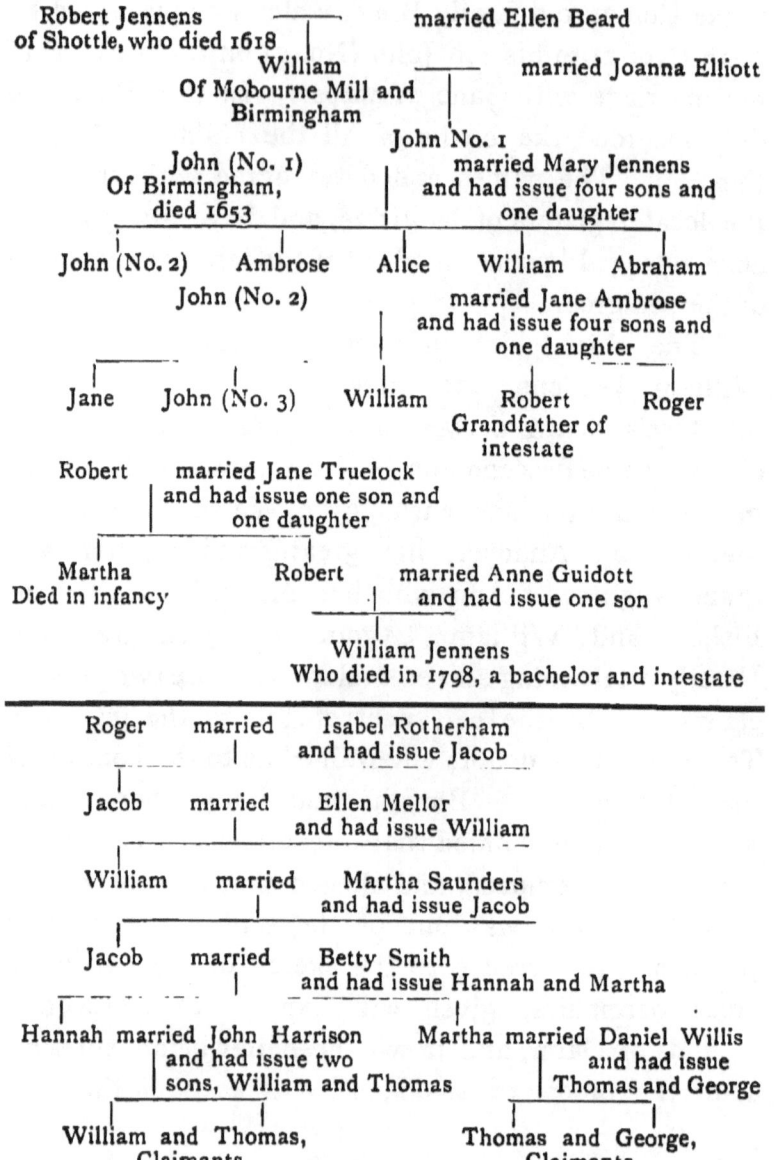

It is a noticeable fact that at the time of his death William Jennens, the intestate, was possessed of all the Jennens' family estates, he having survived all his *then* known relations, and he being then undoubtedly, in the absence of other claims, the heir-at-law.

Soon after the intestate's death Mary Lady Andover and William Lygon appeared as the only next of kin, and succeeded in obtaining administration of the intestate's estate.

As before stated, they claimed to be the only lineal descendants of Humphrey Jennens, the half-brother of John Jennens (No. 2).

The following pedigree shows the descent of the present owners of the property :—

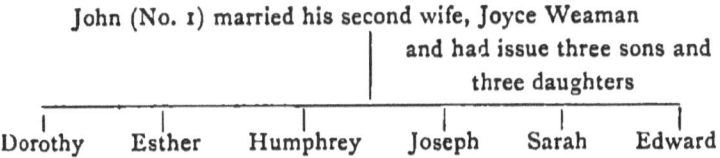

The above-named Humphrey Jennens, the eldest son by the second marriage, is alleged to have been the grandfather of William Jennens, the intestate.

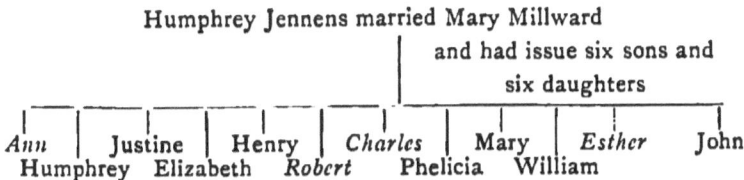

Of these twelve children it will be only necessary for the present to speak of *four*, namely : Ann, the alleged grandmother of Mary Lady Andover; Esther, the alleged grandmother of William Lygon (the administratrix and administrator); Robert, the alleged father of William, the intestate; and Charles, the alleged great-great-grandfather of Earl Howe, who as heir-at-law claimed the real estate.

1st. Ann, daughter of Humphrey Jennens, married Sir Clement Fisher and had issue

Mary who married The Right Hon. Earl of Aylesford and had issue

Mary who married William Howard Viscount Andover, and died either in 1767, 1777 or 1803

2nd. Esther who married William Hanmer and had issue

Susannah who married Reginald Pindar Lygon and had issue

William Lygon who married Catherine Denn
1st Earl Beauchamp   and had issue

William Lygon   John Reginald Pindar Lygon
2nd Earl Beauchamp, died 1823   3rd Earl Beauchamp

3rd. Robert alleged to have married Anne Guidott and to have had issue

William, the intestate

So the descendants of Ann and Esther claimed to be the next of kin to William, the intestate, who was by them represented to be the son of Robert, who was the son of Humphrey.

We next give a sketch pedigree of Earl Howe, who claims to be descended from Charles, one of the sons of Humphrey.

4th.

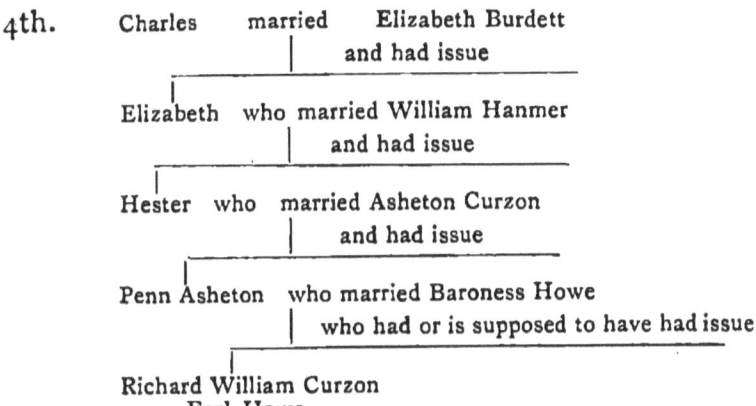

Who as heir-at-law claimed all the real estate.

As regards the latter claim there are many traditions current in the immediate neighbourhood of Acton Place, near Long Melford, which, however, are irrelevant to the present case. Suffice it to say that Earl Howe, if descended from Humphrey Jennens, cannot have a prior right to the claimants, if they and William Jennens, the intestate, can be proved to be descended from John (No. 2), the great-grandfather of the intestate.

To add to the complications of this extraordinary case, there were up to the time of intestate's death five members of the family named *Robert* Jennens or Jennings. By a singular coincidence two of these Robert Jennings resided in London; both of them were married, both of them were very rich, both died in 1725, both left an only son William, neither of these Williams ever married, both of them left fortunes to various members of the Jennings family, one of them died in 1798, and the other in 1803.

It will be the chief care to dissociate these Williams, and to prove the identity of each of them. One of them—he who died in 1798—was the great-grandson of John (No. 2), and the other is believed to have been William, the son of Robert, who was the fourth son of Humphrey Jennens. Even the administratrix and administrator appear to have been in doubt as to the parentage of the intestate; for in the letters of administration (a copy of which will be found hereafter) Robert, the father of William Jennings, the intestate, is described as a WIDOWER, whereas he predeceased his wife, Anne, about thirty-five years. But all the incidents tending to explain these matters will in due course be found in their proper places.

Some of the long wills, together with the pedigrees, will be found in the appendix; but the short wills and other documents of no great length will be embodied in the case.

First, then, is the will of William Jennens, of Birmingham, which is here given *verbatim et literatim* :—

"In the name of God Amen I William Jenins of Birmingham wth in the dioces of Coventry and Lichfielde beinge sicke in body but of goode and pfecte remembrance doe the xxvith day of November Ano dm 1602 make this my last will and testm^t in mann^r and forme followinge first I bequeath my soule to God and

ST. MARTIN'S CHURCH, BIRMINGHAM.

my body to the earthe Itm. touchinge the disposicon of my worldlie goods I give and bequeath them unto Johan Jenins my lovinge wife and thinke they are all little ynoughe for her whom I make my sole executrixe of this my last will and testm^t

"Witnesses hereunto Luke Smythe Clarke Thomas Groves and Thomas Jennens."

Proved 9th Feb$^{y.}$ 1602-3.

The widow of William Jennens appears to have survived her husband twenty years, during which period she made two wills—one in 1612, and another in 1622—both of which were proved, and of which the following are copies (Observe the spelling throughout) :—

"In the name of God Amen I Joane Jennens of Birmingham in the countie of Warwick widdow of the age of seaventie fouer yeares beinge in pfect memory praysed be to the Almightie God doe make and ordeine this my last will and testament first and above all things I bequeath my soule to God Almighty my body to be buryed in the parrish churche of Birmingham to lie so neare as may be to my late husband William Jennens deceased and to have a blue stone layed uppon my grave Now to my worldly goods to despose of as followeth viz. ffirst I doe forgive my sonn Thomas Jennens all debts due to me whatt soe ever be itt by spassuallyte or other wayes and to his daughter Joane three pounds six shillings eight pence to be payed to hir six monethes after my decease to his daughter Mary fortie shillings to his sonn Ambrose fortie shil-

lings to be paide as aforesaide and more to my sonn
Thomas my lesser gilt cupp of plate and after the
decease of Thomas to his sonn Willid Jennens I give to
my daughter An Knight xxd to hir husband Jno. Knight
xx^d to hir daughter An Knight 20^s to hir daughter
Hester Knight xx^s to hir son Thomas Piddock xx^s this
being 5 pounds to be payed six monethes after the decease of my sonn Willid Jennens I give to Joane
Piddock my daughter an daughter In monie tenn
pounds to be payed her vi moneths after the decease of
my sonn William Jennens and more I give to the saide
Joane after my decease one cow wch is at George
Smithies one standing bedsted the feather bed marked
wth a blew rose one bolster one p^r of pillowes two
blanckets one coverlett of 7 or viii^s prise one chest and
one coffer I give to my daughter Mary forte shillings
to hir husband Jno. Stannors twentie shillings and to
hir two sonns xx^s apee being five pounds to be payed
vi monethes after the decease of my sonn Willid
Jennens more to my daughter Mary one cow w^{ch}
shee hath in possession on p^r curteins one close
stoole one warminge pann to be delivered to hir after
my decease I give to my sonn Jno. Jennens five pounds
and to his sonns John and Ambrose fivetie shillings
apeece wch tenn pounds is to be pay^d vi monethes
after the decease of my sonn Willid Jennens I give to
my daughter An and Mary all my waringe clothes in
halves betwene them I give to Mr. Gisborne xi^s after
my decease to be payed I give to my sonn Abraham
Jennens xi^s to his son Abraha to spoons of silver and

guilt to his sonn Ambrose my best beaker of silver and guilt after my decease   More I give to my sonn John Jennens one littell bole and one little beaker after my decease and affter his decease the bole to his sonn John Jennens the beaker to his sonne Ambrose beinge silver I give to my sonn Willid Jennens after my decease thirtie pounds towards his mayntaynance as my executor shall see good soe longe as he shall live I give to Mary Jennens the daughter of my sonn Ambrose two silver spoones to Hester one silver spoone to his daughter Joane two silver spoones to his daughter Susan one silver spoone and to his sonn William Jennens my best silver and guilt bole my will is to have bestowed for the charge of my buriall in giveinge bred to the poore and other ways the some of six pounds thirteene shillings and fouer pence, All my goods unbequeathed I give wth mony chattell w^t soever to my sonn Ambrose Jennens to despose of as he shall see good and heareby this my last will and testament doe ordeine and make him my full and whole executor and for pformance where of I have heare unto sett my hand and seale this p^r sent day beinge the third day of June Anno 1612.

"JOAN × JENNENS

" Witnesses Will Willetts
" Henry Gisborne
" Abra Jennens "

Proved 5th June, 1622.

[In the two foregoing wills it will have been seen that the family name has been spelt "Jenins" "Jennens."]

"In the name of God Amen I Johana Jennens of Birmingham in the countie of Warr. Widdowe of the age of foure skore and three yeares or thereabouts being in pfecte memorie praised be to the Almightie I do hereby make and ordeine this toe to be my last will and testament renounceing and revoking all former wills or grants therby any way maie arise for any former acte of deed done by me ffirst and above all things I bequeathe my soule to God Allmightie Jesus Christe my Savioure and redeemer by whose merrits I hope to be saved my bodie to be bueryed in the Parishe Churche of Birmingham to lye thearsoe neare my late husband William Jennens as convenientlye maye be and theartoe have a blewe stone decentlye toe be laide uppon my grave, Now for my worldly goods I doe dispose by this my last Will and Testament of Vidillicett to Marie the daughter late of Thomas Jennens the some of five pounds and toe Ambrose Jennens her brother fortie shillings toe be paide them sixx mounthes after the decease of my sonne William Jennens more I doe give unto my sonne William Jennens thertie pounds to be into the hands of my executors after my decease presentlye towards the maynetinance and whether the legacies above or theese following are to take place tell that be pformed continewing the naturall life of the said William Jennens more toe my daughter Ann Knight I doe give twentie shillings toe her daughter Johane ffoster fortie shillings and to her daughter Anne and her daughter Hester Knight twentie shillings apeece toe be paide as aforesaide. More I do give to my sonne John

Sonners twentie shillings and his Wyfe my daughter Marie three pounds and for thear toe sonnes John and Thomas twentie shillings apeece toe be paide as aforesaide after the deathe of my sonne William More I doe give toe my sonn *John Jennens tenn pounds and a bowle and a beaker of silver wch are after his decease to be delivered the bowle too his sonn Ambrose and tohis sonn †John Jennens my presse and twentie shillings of monie to his sonn John Jennings and toe William Jennings the beaker sonne to John Jennens and toe his sonn Thomas Jennens fortie shillings I saye fortie shillings to be paide as aforesaide More I do give toe my sonne Ambrose my best silver bowle and toe his chilldren Marie Hester Johane Susann William and Ambrose eache of them a sillver spoone More I do give to my sonne Ambrose my best beaker toe his chilldren Abraham Ambrose Charles William and Judithe eache a sillver spoone apeece and my will is toe have bestowed upon my bueriall in ginge bread to the poore and otherwayes besides the blewe stone the some of sixx pounds therteene shillings foure pence and all my goods unbequeathed I give nowise goods and chattels what soever toe my sonne Ambrose Jennens whom I make my full executor toe dispose of as he shall thincke fitt and if the saide Ambrose die then my sonne Abraham toe stand my executor as aforesaide and if the bothe departe then my sonne John to be in forme as aforesaide further all my wearinge

---
* John Jennens (No. 1).
† John Jennens (No. 2).

clothes I doe give toe be delivered equallie to my daughter Ann Knight and Marie Stanners thoughe theese be nott all togeather soe directlye as by lawe maye be expressed yett I doe hereby ordeyne and my will is that this shall stand for my last will and testamente in as full force as anye writting can be made In witness hereof I have heareuntoe puttoe my hande and seale this twentehe seventhe daie of Maye 1618."

" Further my meaning is that the over plusse of the thertie pounds reserved for my sonn William of suche monie goods as shalbe founde shalbe paide out wth in six mounthes after my decease when my executor shall thincke most neede the plate and spoones to eache partie are to be delivered soe soone as maie convenientlye maye be more I doe give to my daughter Marie Stanners my warminge pann a paire of greene curtaines and a chamber stoole. In wittness of this writting I the aforesaide Johane Jennens have hereunto sett my hand and seale the day and yeare above written.

" Sealed and delived in the psents
of us under written
" ABRAHAM JENNENS
" JOHN JENNENS."

Proved 10th July, 1622.

These wills sufficiently prove that William Jennens, of Birmingham, the husband of Joanna Jennings, the testatrix, was the father of John Jennens (No. 1) and the grandfather of his son John (No. 2).

It was this John (No. 2) who married Jane Ambrose, and was the father of Roger Jennings (see pedigree).

INTERIOR OF ST. MARTIN'S CHURCH, BIRMINGHAM.

The will of John Jennens (No. 1), which is too long for insertion here, but a copy of which will be found in the appendix, is dated 25th February, 1651. This was the year when Cromwell became Protector, and the country throughout was still in an unsettled state. John Jennens (No. 2) appears to have been, at this time, residing at Mobourne Mill, and his son John (No. 3), who was only 11 years of age, would be living with his father at Mobourne Mill, Duffield.

John Jennens (No. 1), by his will, after giving directions for his burial, devises the dwelling-house, in which he then dwelt at Birmingham, together with the appurtenances, and all the croft or close near the new street in Birmingham, purchased by him of William Ward, with the appurtenances; also all that parcel of land at the lower end of testator's garden, then lately purchased by Robert Baylies; and also all that croft or close of pasture, commonly called Maddocke Croft, in or near the new street aforesaid; and also all that close or pasture, commonly called Colehouse, with the appurtenances; and all those three closes or parcels of land, commonly called Hungerhills, at Edgbaston, in the county of Warwick, unto his son Humphrey Jennens and the heirs of his body; and for the want of such issue, then he gives and devises the said Colehouse and Hungerhills* to his son Joseph Jennens and the heirs of his body, and for want of such issue, to his son Edward Jennings and the heirs of his body, and for the want of such issue, "To the heirs of my bodie on the

---
* As to the Colehouse and Hungerhill Estate at Edgbaston.

bodie of my late deare tender wife Joyce Jennens, lawfully to be begotten" and for want of such issue "to the right heirs of me the said John Jennens for ever."

And for want of the heirs of the body of Humphrey Jennens, testator gives the said messuage and lands in Birmingham unto his son Edward Jennens and the heirs of his body, and for want of such issue, to his son Joseph Jennens and the heirs of his body, and for the want of such issue "to the heires of my bodie and the bodye of my said Wiefe Joyce Jennens lawfully to be begotten," and for want of such issue "to my right heyres for ever." Testator then gives and devises all those his several leases, estates, interests, and terms of years then yet to come, of or in a certain meadow commonly called Barnes Meadow, lying and being in Duddeston, in the county of Warwick; and in certain barns, crofts, closes and lands in Birmingham, which testator then held of Robert Phillipps; and also in certain parcels of meadow ground in Codington, in Warwick, which testator then held of Ambrose Phillipps; and also a certain house in Birmingham, which testator held of the Governors of the Free School of Birmingham, unto his son Humphrey Jennens, his executors, administrators and assigns, subject to the covenants and conditions in the said several leases contained. Then there is a conditional bequest of £500 to testator's daughter Sarah, with remainder (if any) to testator's children, Humphrey, Joseph and Edward. Testator also gives to his three sons, Humphrey, Joseph and Edward Jennens, his several estates, leases, interests,

and terms of years yet to come, of or in the forges,
water-courses and highway, and Aston furnace, with all
edifices and appurtenances at Hales, in the county of
Stafford, and in Curdington and Aston (with certain
quantities of charcoal and pig-iron), subject to the
covenants and conditions in the said several leases
thereof contained. Testator then gives to his son
Edward, his executors, administrators and assigns, all
his leasehold estates at Westbury, West Bromwich and
Walsall, in the county of Stafford, subject to the terms
of lease and to the tenant-right of John Carter, the
under-lessee. The testator then refers to an advance-
ment to his son Abraham; he then gives him, by conditional bequest, the annual income arising from an
investment of £350 for life, with remainder to Abraham's
children, and for want of lawful issue, to the heirs of
testator's body on the body of his dear and tender wife,
Joyce Jennens, and for want of such issue, to his own
right heirs for ever. Then follow a further conditional
bequest of £50 and £20. Then follow certain directions for investing certain portions of his personal estate
for the purpose of buying gowns and coats for poor inhabitants of Birmingham, the same to be bought and provided at Christide for ever. Testator then gives to his
mother-in-law, Dorothy, £3, to buy her a gown.* "Item
I give unto my daughter-in-law Jane Jennens† five
pounds to buy her a goune and to John Jennens sonne

---

* Bequest to Dorothy, the mother of testator's first wife, Mary Jennens.

† Bequest to Jane Jennens, formerly Jane Ambrose.

of my late sonne John Jennens* five pounds to be payed unto him at hys age of one and twentie years Item I give unto my grande childe Jane Jennens† when shee shalbe of the age of eighteen yeares tenn pounds and to my grande childe William Jennens‡ when he shalbe of the age of one and twentie yeares tenn pounds." Then there is a bequest to the wife of Abraham Jennens of £5, and to Abraham's son John £20, and to Joyce, Abraham's daughter, £10, and to Alice, her sister, £5. Then follow bequests to testator's god-children and servants. Residue of estate to be divided into four equal parts, and one moiety or half to be paid to testator's son Humphrey Jennens, and the other moiety or half to and among testator's children, Joseph, Edward and Sarah; to his overseers, 40s. a-piece. The will was proved at Westminster, on the 10th March, 1653, by the sole executor, Humphrey Jennens.

From the foregoing will it has been seen that testator has shewn great partiality to the children by his second marriage. He leaves only nominal legacies to his son John's children, namely to Jane, John and William. No mention is made of his son John's two other children Robert and Roger. This it must be admitted is unfortunate, and such omission may have been occasioned by testator's belief that his son John was dead, or it may have been an eccentric affectation merely by reason of some imagined slight or political

---

* Bequest to John Jennens (No. 3).

† Bequest to Jane, the eldest child of John Jennens (No. 2).

disobedience. Fathers, sons and brothers, and other near kinsmen then entertained opposite views, and frequently met and fought on the field of battle. Such were the lamentable consequences of civil wars. Even in our own day it has not unfrequently happened that an angry parent has without good reason assumed a child to be dead, and forbidden his or her name to be ever mentioned, the result of which has been, that such an event has by the rest of the family been tacitly admitted to have taken place. Or it may have been the selfish and subtle suggestion of Mr. Weaman, the solicitor who prepared the will, with the intention to aggrandize as much as he could of testator's property for the benefit of his own grand-children, they being the testator's children by the second marriage. They who disbelieve in the reasonableness of any of these theories, or who are still sceptical as to the existence of John (No. 2) at the time of the date of the will, ought in all fairness to produce some evidence in support of their views; and the only accurate testimony they can obtain is the certificate of his burial at an earlier date. This they cannot produce. But in the register at Duffield there is the record of the burial of John (No. 2), on the 31st of January, 1673.

If then John (No. 2) survived his father John (No. 1) and the old Family Bible be admissible in evidence, as without doubt it will be, then the paternity of Robert Jennens, the grandfather of William Jennens the intestate, as also that of Roger Jennens, will be fully

John Jennens (No. 2) was baptised on the 8th March, 1607, and was married in 1636 to Jane Ambrose, in East Garston Church, in Berkshire. The entries of marriages from the year 1564 to 1661 have at some time been cut out of the Register of East Garston Church. A certificate, of which the following is a copy, has been given to that effect :—

"I, Leverson C. Randolph, vicar of East Garston, Berkshire, do certify that the entries of marriages in the Parish Register Book of East Garston from the year 1564 to 1661 have been at some time cut out from the Parish Register Book, and have no doubt that the Ambrose family resided at Maidencourt in this parish, and John Jennings and Jane Ambrose were probably married at East Garston Church.

"(Signed) LEVERSON C. RANDOLPH."

Two affidavits have been filed to the following effect—

William Boucher of Eastbury, near Lambourne, Hungerford (about 7 miles from Reading), says as follows :—

"That he is 76 years of age, and several years ago kept a public house near Reading. He has often heard both his father and uncle say that the Ambrose family intermarried with the Birmingham Jennings, and that John Jennings and Jane Ambrose were married in East Garston Church."

The other affidavit is as follows :—

"That I am the vicar of East Garston Church, and that I have been vicar there   years."

" That in or about the month of May, 1865, I was applied to by Mr. William Bennett for a certificate of the marriage of John Jennens and Jane Ambrose, who, I was informed, formerly resided at Reading. That on searching the parish register books for such certificate, I found that the entries of marriage from the year 1564 to 1661 had been cut out from such register. That I believe from the present appearance of the register that the leaves of the said register had been surreptitiously cut away for the purpose of concealing some particular certificate or certificates of marriage, but whether the same had been cut away at one or at several different times I am unable to state as to my belief or otherwise. That having been informed that the said certificate was sought for the purpose of establishing the fact that one John Jennens, of Birmingham, married a Jane Ambrose of Maidencourt, East Garston, Berkshire; and my assistance having been requested to further that end, I made enquiries, and was informed by an old inhabitant named William Boucher, residing near East Garston, that there was a family named Ambrose living at Maidencourt Farm about the year 1636, and that one of these named Jane married a John Jennings, who came from Birmingham, and that he and his wife subsequently lived at Reading, and that the said John Jennings was elected Mayor of Reading.

"That I entertain no doubt from the information I have received that the Ambrose family resided in East Garston, Berkshire. That the said Jane Ambrose married the said John Jennings in East Garston Church, and that the said John Jennings was the same John Jennings or Jennens, of Birmingham, referred to by the beforenamed William Boucher, and also that this John Jennings was elected Mayor of Reading on the 26th day of August, 1639.

"That the said John Jennings and Jane Jennings his wife (formerly Jane Ambrose) lived at Reading in the year 1639, and that they were respectively the John Jennens, of Birmingham, and in the bill of complaint in the abovenamed suit referred to as John Jennens, the son, and Jane Ambrose, of East Garston."

Jane, John (No. 3), William, Robert, and Roger, were the issue of this marriage. Jane died unmarried in 1663. The descendants of John (No. 3) have failed in proving him to be their ancestor; in fact, the case has never been properly before the court. William's line is known to be extinct. Robert was entered at the Middle Temple in 1649, at the early age of five years, in accordance with the then prevailing custom. The entry is as follows—" Robert Jennens, second son of John Jennings, late of Redding, in the County of Berks, gentleman." This Robert Jennens, then, was the son of John Jennens (No. 2); he was born at Mobourne Mill on the 9th July, 1644; entered at Middle

Temple in November, 1649; married Jane Truelock, at Aldworth, in Berkshire, in 1669; and had issue one son, Robert, and one daughter, Martha. The latter died in infancy. His son, Robert, was born in 1672; he married Anne Guidott in 1700, and had issue one child only, the late William Jennens, of Acton Place, Suffolk, who died in 1798 a bachelor and intestate. The repetition now and then of some portions of the pedigree will be found to be absolutely necessary to avoid confusion and error. Roger's descendants will, therefore, be the legal claimants.

Notwithstanding the partial destruction of the marriage register at East Garston, it was considered that the transcripts would be preserved in the Diocesan Registry at Salisbury. Here accordingly search was made, and but one transcript for a portion of the year 1636 could be found. It was explained that the imperfect state of the transcripts was possibly due to accidents. The roads at that time were difficult and dangerous to travel, the visitations were irregular, and sometimes the churchwardens were negligent or perhaps too unwell to perform their duties. All the transcripts of marriages, all the marriage bonds and marriage license books for the years 1635 to 1639 inclusive have been searched, but in vain. But the transcripts being written on several pieces of parchment and filed on a string, it may be that at some time they have become loose and misplaced, or been lost, or stolen probably during the occupation of the Cathedral by the Parliamentary troops during the Civil War.

One proof that Robert Jennens, the father of the late William Jennens the intestate, was not the fourth son of Humphrey Jennens as alleged, is furnished by the office copy will of Mary Jennens, one of the daughters of the said Humphrey Jennens. If, indeed, he were the fourth son of Humphrey Jennens, then he and Mary Jennens were *brother* and *sister*. Please bear this in mind.

The will of Mary Jennens bears date the 29th September, 1708. This, however, seems to be a mere clerical error. The date should be 1707, since the will was proved on the 4th January, 1708. In her will, testatrix mentions her brothers John, Humphrey, Robert and William. These are parties interested in the will, and, therefore, should be considered as disqualified to act as witnesses. But it becomes necessary to prove the handwriting of testatrix, and a Robert Jennens and Anne, his wife, are called upon to prove it. Appended to the office copy will is the identification of Mary Jennens' handwriting by Robert Jennens, and Anne, his wife. The question to be decided is, is the witness Robert Jennens the same person as Robert Jennens named in the will; and is the language of Robert Jennens the witness, the language of a brother identifying his sister's handwriting. The reader will judge for himself. The following is a copy :—

"4th Jan$^{y.}$ 1708.

" Which day appeared personally Robert Jennens of the parish of St. Andrews Holborne in the county of Middlesex Esq. and Anne Jennens of the same parish and alleadged that they were well acquainted with the testatrix Mary Jennens deceased for *several years* before her death and that by their frequent conversation and often seeing her write became very well acquainted with her manner and character of handwriting and verily believe in their consciences that the testamentary schedule hereunto annexed was totally wrote with the proper handwriting of the said testatrix.—'Robert Jennens' 'Anne Jennens.'"

" Dicti Robertus Jennens et Anna Jennens jurate fuerunt super veritate premissorum coram me Gul. Willymott sue p^c sente. Tho. Willymott Reis Pubro."

Had the witness Robert Jennens been really the brother of Mary Jennens, the testatrix, one would suppose he would have said so; but here his language is that of an acquaintance, or at the most of a distant relative.

This Robert Jennens died suddenly in Holborn in 1725 or 6, the date being variously given in the pedigrees, and he was buried in Acton Church, in Suffolk. His widow, Anne Jennens, survived him 35 years. In 1726, William Jennens, the intestate, made a will in favour of his mother, and in his will he refers to his late father. Yet we find that in 1803 Administration de bonis non of the said Robert Jennens' estate and effects was granted to William Lygon, Esq., and in the Letters of Administration the said Robert Jennens is described as a *widower*.

It has been previously stated that the late William Jennens, the intestate, survived all his *then* known relatives, and it may readily be presumed that William Lygon was either ignorant of the real state of things, or wilfully perpetrated a wicked and deliberate fraud.

That the late Lady Mary Andover was equally as careless or as culpable can be easily proved. See her letters to Mrs. Anne Patrick.

If, then, the claimants be in a position to prove either a fraud or a trust, it is to be hoped they will succeed.

Fraud has been defined to be, "All deceitful practices in defrauding or endeavouring to defraud another of his known right by means of some artful device, contrary to the plain rule of common honesty." It is a rule, however, in Equity that fraud is not to be presumed. It must be proved by the acts done, and the consequences. If by suppressing the truth, or by suggesting a falsehood, *or even by a fraudulent silence*, the parties managed to secure the property to themselves, there is still hope for redress, for proceedings can be taken for discovery of the fraud, and in such instances the Statutes of Limitation can never be pleaded in Bar.

As regards a trust, what can be more explicit than the 36 and 37 Vict., c. 66, s. 25, sub-s. 2—"No claim of a cestui que trust against his trustee for any property held on an express trust, or in respect of any breach of such trust, shall be held to be barred by any Statute of Limitations."

A further affidavit was filed, of which the following is a copy:—

"I Elizabeth Somerton of Somerton in the parish of Somerton in the County of Oxford Widow make oath and say:—

"1.—That I was born on the 11th day of Octr 1778 and was married about the year 1817 to Mr. William Somerton of Somerton aforesaid since deceased.

"2.—That I am the daughter of William Jennings of Somerton aforesaid farmer and Land Surveyor and the granddaughter of James Jennings of Somerton aforesaid Land Surveyor also deceased.

"3.—That when I was about 4 years of age my father the before-named William Jennings died and I was brought up with my uncle James Jennings my said father's brother at Somerton aforesaid.

"4.—That my grandfather James Jennings being a Land Surveyor brought up his two sons to the same business and they used to survey estates for the late William Jennens Esq. of Acton near Long Melford in the County of Suffolk deceased the intestate in the pleadings of this cause named my uncle and grandfather were upon the best and most familiar terms with the said William Jennens and on various occasions they visited at each other's house which accounted for the said William Jennens visiting Somerton.

" 5.—That I well remember when I was young that the said William Jennens frequently came to my uncle's house, and I have frequently heard my grandfather James Jennings and William (meaning the said William Jennens) conversing about his father Robert and how he the said Robert was left an orphan when he was very young about 12 years old as near as I can remember and that his the said Robert's father and mother and his sister Martha were buried at Sutton Courtney in the County of Berks. and that Robert was sent to London to live with Edward Jennings of the Inner Temple and resided there till his marriage with Anne Guidott a rich lady and that he sold his property at Sutton Courtney in the County of Berks. after he bought the estates in Suffolk and Essex.

" 6.—I further say that I so well remember the said William Jennens visiting Somerton that I can describe the dress he wore on his last visit *videlicit* a high hat and a grey coat and he carried a gold-headed cane and he said to me ' Betsy you must be a good girl and then I shall remember you.' I was about 18 years old at that time."

To prove beyond all doubt that John (No. 1), of Birmingham, was mistaken as to the death of his son

John (No. 2), it will be necessary to refer to the proceedings in the suit, John Jennens v. Roger Norton, filed in or about the year 1646. In his bill of complaint John Jennens (No. 1) refers to the death of his son John (No. 2), and alleges that Roger Norton applied for and took letters of administration in trust for John Jennens (No. 1) and one Hester Jennens the widow of his late brother Ambrose Jennens.

Now it will be seen on referring to the pedigree that William Jennens of Mobourne Mill had two sons named Ambrose and John. These two brothers carried on business in co-partnership together, Ambrose conducting a branch business in London, whilst John remained in Birmingham. Ambrose died, leaving his widow Hester Jennens, who continued to carry on her husband's business in co-partnership with her brother-in-law John Jennens (No. 1). John Jennens (No. 2) also went to London and conducted an agency in connection with the joint trade of John and Hester Jennens. In the bill of complaint it is alleged that John (No. 2) had then been dead about two years; Hester Jennens died and her will was duly proved by Roger Norton her executor, who in that capacity sued John Jennens (No. 1) for the balance due from the partnership to the estate of Hester Jennens, and John Jennens (No. 1) then sought relief in equity

Roger Norton filed his answer, and in it he denies in general terms the whole of the allegations set forth in the bill of complaint.

The following are extracts from the documents now in the possession of the claimants, and it is assumed they are correct :—
" To the Right Honourable the Commissioners
for the Great Seal of England.
" In humble manner complaining sheweth unto your honours your daily Orator John Jennens of Birmingham in the County of Warwick Ironmonger. That whereas about 30 years since one Ambrose Jennens of London since deceased late brother unto your Orator had in trading and dealing together with your Orator for   thousand pounds in divers and several ironwares and commodities of divers and several sorts in hand-irons which from time to time your Orator bought in the Country and sent the same to London to the said Ambrose where he sold the same by means whereof the said Ambrose did gain and raise to himself a great personal estate and in or about the year of our Lord 1626 died possessed of such an estate as aforesaid after whose decease, all accounts being fully and perfectly cleared and set straight between them one Hester Jennens since deceased the then relict of the said Ambrose Jennens did by and much importunity so far prevail with your Orator for the continuing the said joint trade with her the said Hester as that your Orator was therewith content. And thereupon your Orator sheweth that in or about September which was in the third yeare of his Majestie's reign that now is and in the year of our Lord God 1627 there were certain Indentures or Articles of Agreement or Co-partnership

TOWN HOUSE OF JOHN JENNENS, BIRMINGHAM, 1653.

in writing had and made by and between your Orator
and the said Hester when by it, it was agreed to such
or the like effect following namely. That your Orator
and the said Hester should be from thenceforth Co-
partners together in the buying selling or trading of
for or concerning the said Ironwares for the term of 7
years and that the said Hester and your said Orator
should put in and accordingly they did put in each of
them £1000 a piece to be used and employed as a joint
stock in the said trade for and during the said term.
And moreover it was truly intended and agreed that
what profit loss or gain were or should be had or made
in or by the said trade either by buying or selling during
the said Co-partnership should be equally paid borne
and discharged by and between your Orator and the
said Hester and also all other charges in losses for or
concerning the said trade to be equally paid borne and
discharged by or between your Orator and the said
Hester. And Moreover it was agreed and by and
through the earnest request and desire of the said
Hester that the managing of the said trade should be
committed to your Orator and in regard she the said
Hester and the said Ambrose her said late husband
had for many years together gained and got great
benefit and advantage in and by your Orator's dealing
as aforesaid thereupon the said Hester was content
and moreover it was agreed in or about September 1630
that the said Hester should add and putt into the said
joint stock £300 more over and besides her said £1000
which by agreement was to be and remain a dead stock
as unto her the said Hester and for which she should

have no benefit or advantage in or during the time that the said joint trade should continue between them save only that it was agreed that your Orator should give and accordingly did give the said Hester security by his bond bearing date on or about the 23 day of Sepr. 1630. conditioned for the repayment of the said £300 within 6 months next after Michaelmas 1635 or within 6 months next after the decease of the said Hester Jennens or within 6 months next after the death of your said Orator which should first or next happen. At the expiration of the term of Co-partnership for 7 years the said Hester finding and perceiving what great profit and gains she had yearly made and received earnestly did desire and move that their Co-partnership might continue or be renewed for 7 years longer upon such or the like terms and conditions for your Orator did from time to time and every year give and make with the said Hester Jennens a true and perfect account in writing of or concerning the said tradings and it was expressly agreed by the said Hester that any losses or damages which in any of the said years should happen that the same should be by her afterwards allowed unto your Orator, And by the request and earnest importunity of the said Hester Jennens your Orator did condition that the said joint trade and co-partnership should continue between them for 7 years longer and new Articles of Agreement or Indentures were made between them in or about September in the 11th year of his Majestie's reign upon such or the like terms and conditions of the former Agreement which said Articles of Agreement did determine in or about September 1642.

And it was also agreed that the said £300 should remain and continue as a dead stock as in the former Agreement, And your Orator did from year to year give and make unto the said Hester an account of the said joint trade the hazard and losses to be borne equally between them. But now so it is that the said Co-partnership being ended and the said Hester Jennens being dead who died about 15 months since and having made her last Will and Testament in writing and made one Roger Norton of Blackfriars London Printer, who married one of the daughters of the said Hester her executor he the said Roger having the said Will and taken upon himself the execution thereof and having got the said Indentures of Co-partnership which are under the hand of your said Orator and the several accounts which your Orator from tyme to tyme made and gave to the said Hester and knowing that the said Orator was plundered of several writings relating to the said Co-partnership by the Soldiers and other Forces which were under the command of Prince Rupert when they were at Birmingham aforesaid since the beginning of these troublesome times.* And the said Roger Norton taking advantage thereof hath not only and of late denyed that the said Indentures of Agreement were to any such effect or purpose as aforesaid or that the said Hester Jennens was thereby to pay or discharge any part or loss of any ill debt losses or other charges of or concerning the said joint trade. And the said Roger Norton hath refused to allow pay or beare his proportionable part or share of or concerning all such

---

* In a similar way several Registers were destroyed.

doubtful or desperate debts concerning the said joint trade by and from the several persons hereafter following—from Ambrose Jennens £9 14s. 8d. (and others) all such the said debts amounting in the whole to the sum of £1500 or thereabouts. And your Orator hath at several times offered and desired the said Roger Norton to come to a just and fair account all which the said Roger Norton hath refused and doth yet refuse to allowe or pay. All which said premises are well known unto the said Roger Norton and your Orator showeth that in or by two several accounts indented were had made and cast up between your Orator and the said Hester Jennens and whereunto the said Roger was privy and also a Witness and whereunto he subscribed his hand the one bearing date on or about the 13th Sepr 1641 and the other about September 1642. And moreover your Orator sheweth that the said Hester Jennens for about 20 years last past before her death did maintain a lecture in Birmingham aforesaid, the same being a Market Town, namely two sermoms in every month which cost her £10 per annum and in regard your Orator did dwell in Birmingham aforesaid and the said Hester in London aforesaid she the said Hester did from time to time by letters and otherwise desire your Orator for and on her behalf to pay the said £10 per annum for and in discharge of the said lecture which your said Orator did for about 18 years and the said Hester did never give or make your said Orator any recompense or satisfaction of or concerning the same, And that the said Roger Norton who hath heard the said Hester Jennens confess and acknowledge the same and having sufficient assets in his hands to pay and satisfy the said just debts of the said Hester Jennens is and ought to pay and satisfy the same unto your Orator. And moreover your Orator sheweth that in and during the time of the said joint trade and co-partnership as aforesaid it was agreed by and between your Orator and the said Hester that your Orator should from time to time send and consign divers and several ironwares and commodities of all sorts from Birmingham aforesaid to London aforesaid to John Jennens since deceased your Orator's son and that the said John Jennens should drive the trade in his own name and should from time to time sell and dispose the said goods to such person or persons as he should think fit which should be in trust nevertheless to and for the equal use and benefit of your Orator and of the said Hester And your Orator sheweth that the said John Jennens your Orator's said late son did sell divers and several of the said goods and ironwares to divers and several persons upon trust and did take several bills or other security in his own name and several sums of money were due and owing unto him at the time of his decease which were due unto the said joint trade the particulars whereof may appear in and by several book or books of account which he had or did keep for that purpose. All which since the decease of the said John Jennens are come to the hands of the said Roger Norton or of some other person or persons to his use and acknowledge and the said Roger Norton who well knowed the premises to be true hath since the decease

E

of the said John Jennens your Orator's son who died
in or about two years since possessed of a good personal
Estate as in his own right amounting to a good value
and possessed likewise of a personal estate for a joint
and equal use of your said Orator and the said Hester
amounting likewise to a good value taken letters of
Administration of all and singular his said goods
chattels rights and credits but before such time as
your Orator did or would permit or suffer him to take
the same it was agreed by and between your Orator
and the said Roger Norton that the said Roger Norton
should have and take the letters of Administration in
trust nevertheless and for the joint and equal use and
benefit of your said Orator and of the said Hester
whereby the said debts so due in equity to the said
joint trade might be the better got in and received and
accordingly disposed of for the joint and equal use and
benefit of your Orator and of the Estate of the said
Hester, and accordingly he the said Roger Norton hath
lately and since possessed himself of all and singular
the said personal estate of the said John Jennens and of
all his books of accounts and hath since his decease had
and received divers and several sums of money which
were due and owing to the said John Jennens at the
time of his decease. In tender consideration of all
which premises and for that your Orator hath no
remedy by the Common Laws of this Realm to be
relieved in or against the same or the aforesaid several
extremities and indirect proceedings of the said Roger
Norton and to enforce him to produce the said several
Indentures of Co-partnership, and the several accounts

and other writings whereby the truth thereof may appear, etc.

"And your Orator shall ever pray, etc."

To which Bill of Complaint of John Jennens the said Roger Norton answers as follows.

" November 1646.

" The Defendant sayeth that he did never know the said Ambrose Jennens deceased in the Bill named or what dealings he the said Ambrose had with the Complainant John Jennens nor doth he know when the said Ambrose died or of what he died possessed nor whether the said Hester relict of the said Ambrose did prevail on the said Complainant to continue the said trade in Co-partnership and also denies or objects to the Complaints set forth in the Bill."

From the foregoing extracts of Bill of Complaint and Answer, it is evident that Ambrose and John (No. 1) were brothers; that their joint trade was carried on by Ambrose in London, and by John in Birmingham; that John, of Birmingham, had a son John (No. 2), who carried on a business in London in his own name, in trust for the said co-partnership, after the death of Ambrose Jennings; that John (No. 2) had been missing or been thought to be dead two years or more before anyone administered his estate. John (No. 1) was no doubt a very prudent man, and he would of course so manage the business as to lessen the risk of war. Hence, perhaps, the concealed trust whereby John (No. 2) not only enriched himself but realized something handsome for his principals. But why such delay in administering the estate? It is more than probable that John (No. 2) was about 1642 or 1644 induced to leave London in consequence of his political opinions. The Civil War had been raging two years, and it was difficult for any man under the circumstances to remain neutral. John (No. 1) we may suppose to have been a Republican, since he complains of having been plundered by the soldiers under Prince Rupert, treatment he would not have received at their hands had he been a Royalist. It does not appear whether John (No. 2) was a Republican or a Royalist, but according to the traditions of the family he, during the Civil War, suddenly left London and retired with his family to Mobourne Mill, where he remained till the day of his death. No certificate of his death can be found prior to 1673; and since Roger Norton denies generally the allegations in the above-mentioned bill of complaint, it may be concluded that John (No. 2) was desirous of concealment only, and that for reasons best known to himself, he lived there in seclusion and estranged to all the family except his wife and children. Wherever he went to live after his marriage with Jane Ambrose, he appears to have taken the Family Bible with him,—first to Reading, where he resided from 1636 to 1641, during which time he became the Mayor of that town; then to Birmingham, to assist his father; then to London, to carry on business for his father and his aunt on trust; and then to Mobourne Mill, at that time a beautiful sylvan retreat, and well adapted for the purpose of concealment.

The further history of the Family Bible will be given hereafter.

We will now proceed with the pedigree of John (No. 2). He had five children, namely:—Jane, who was born either at Reading or Birmingham in 1637, and died unmarried. John, who was born and baptised at Birmingham in 1640, and died in 1710. William, who was born and baptised at Birmingham in 1643, married and had issue one child, which died in infancy; William and his wife and child were buried at Hales Owen, in Salop. Robert, born and baptised at Duffield in 1644, and died at Aldworth, in Berkshire, in 1686. Roger who was born and baptised at Duffield in 1653, and died at Duffield in 1712.

As it is to John (No. 3) and to his descendants that the claimants are indebted for the preservation of the Family Bible, their account of the Bible, being handed down from generation to generation, will be offered as an additional proof on behalf of the present claimants.

John (No. 3) was as has been said a Quartermaster in the Parliamentary army. He appears to have been appointed at the early age of 19. The following is a copy of the original letter written to him by General Monk :—

"George Monk, Captain General and Commander-in-Chief of all the forces in England, Scotland and Ireland.
"To John Jennings, Quartermaster.
"To Mark Woodall, junr.,
"Birmingham.
"By virtue of the power and authority to me given

I do hereby constitute and appoint you John Jennings to be Quartermaster to Captain Strangeway's Troop in Colonel Matthew Aherca's Regiment, raised and main to you under my command for the service of the Parliament and Commonwealth of England. You are therefore to take unto your charge and care the said Troop as Quartermaster thereof, and duly exercise the Officers and Soldiers of the same in arms, and also to do your best care and endeavour to keep them in good order and discipline, commanding them to obey you as their Quartermaster. And you are likewise to follow and observe such orders and directions as you shall from time to time receive from the Parliament Council of State, appointed by Parliament, or myself. And also you are to obey the superior Officers of the Regiment and Army according to the discipline of War, in pursuance of the trust reposed in you and your duty to the Parliament and Commonwealth of England.

"Given under my hand and seal at St. James', the 25th day of February, 1659.

"(Signed) "GEORGE MONK."

In the following year John (No. 3) was married to Dorothy Bridgens, at Birmingham, and in the same year King Charles II. was restored to the throne. John (No. 3) thereupon immediately left England, and was engaged in foreign service until the accession of William III., when he returned, having been absent from his wife 28 years. He and his wife were still only about 48 years of age. In 1688 they had issue one child—Mary. At that time John (No. 3) resided at Duddeston Hall, near Birmingham, an estate which he had acquired by descent from Mary Jennens, his grandmother, the first wife of John (No. 1). Here he continued to live until shortly after the marriage of his daughter to James Essex, who was a miller employed on the estate and with whom Mary Jennings eloped. He (John No. 3) then sold Duddeston Hall, and removed to Saltley Hall. He died in 1710 leaving all his estate, to his daughter Mary Essex, who after her father's death and until the death of her husband, which took place in 1721, continued to reside there. Mary Essex the widow then married John Handy, who being an improvident man soon reduced his wife and family to a state of poverty. By her first marriage with James Essex there were four children, one being named Mary: by her second marriage there was one child. All these children save Mary Essex died in infancy. John (No. 3) had possession of the Family Bible, and by him it was left to his daughter Mary, who gave it to her daughter Mary, by whom it was placed in a box containing a few relics of the former respectability of the family. Part of these family relics consist of elaborately embroidered silk dresses, which must have been purchased at very great cost, and a few articles of jewellery, including a Freemason's Medal. Mary Essex, the granddaughter of John (No. 3), married John Blyth and by him had issue four children, namely—Thomas, Ann, Elizabeth and Hannah.

Thomas Blyth the eldest child and only son married Mary Sherwood, and had issue a child named Mary, who married Samuel Baylis and had issue a child named Samuel, who married Charlotte Whitehouse and had issue James Baylis, who is now living.

Ann Blyth, the second child of John and Mary Blyth, married Thomas Patrick and died without issue.

Elizabeth Blyth, the third child of John and Mary Blyth, married Isaac Perry and had issue Mary, who married Joseph Biggs and had issue Eliza, now the wife of William Rhodes, of Birmingham.

The box containing the family relics came ultimately into the possession of Eliza, the wife of William Rhodes. For many years it was kept in a garret unnoticed, but had often been the subject of conversation with the members of the family. There were also many papers which afterwards were entrusted to the care of Thomas Patrick, who disposed of them without the sanction of the family. (See copies of Affidavits in Appendix.) The box and its contents were at one time much damaged on account of the defective state of the roof, and they were then carefully examined. Happily the Bible was not much injured, and the entries, although they have become faint by damp and age, are still legible. The style and character of the writing, as also the spelling, will be fair subjects for comment; but it must be remembered that education two hundred years ago was greatly neglected by the middle classes, and that even among the superior classes no uniformity of spelling was recognized.

The word "marriage" appears to be spelt "marridge," but the upper stroke of the "d" may have been caused by a want of control over the pen; but the substitution of "Boy" for "By" is the phonetic style of the time.

The following is a copy of the entries in the Family Bible :—
"This Book was given to John Jennens at his marridge May 15 1636 boy his
"Father John Jennens.
"Jane Born May 10 1637.
"John Born March 22 1640.
"William Born Jenuary 2 1643.
"Robert Born July 9 1644.
"Rodger Born November 6 1653.
"John Jennens married to
"Dorethy Bridgons Oct. 2 1660
"Mary Born July 30 1688."

[The above entries are all on the inside of one of the covers of the Bible. The following is a copy of the entries on the other side] :—
"Married 29th January 1708.
"James Essex to Mary Jennens.
"Anne born November 10 1710.
"John born September 20 1712.
"Mary born January 12 1714.
"James born September 29 1717.
"Second marriage to
"John*   dy October 26 1724.
"William born Novmber 12 1733.
"Married
†"John Blythe to Mary Essex December 9 1736.

---

* This blank is caused by damp, part of the name "Handy" being worn away.
† Daughter of J. and M. Essex.

It is surprising that the mere misspelling of a word and that word a Christian name, was as recently as April, 1836, deemed conclusive evidence against the Plaintiff, in the suit " Hood *v.* Beauchamp." In this case Mary Hood was the representative of Sarah King, who was alleged to be the sole next of kin of William Jennens the intestate. The suit was instituted against the personal representatives of William Jennens, who were the late Lady Andover and the late Lord Beauchamp, and the object of the Plaintiff was to prove that she was related to William Jennens, the intestate, in a nearer degree than that of the Defendant. The case submitted to the court was simply this : Humphrey Jennens, the brother of John (No. 2), had a daughter named Elizabeth, who was born some time between the baptism of Mary, in 1664, and John, in 1667, but who, from having married a person in a humble class of life, and embraced the Roman Catholic religion, ceased to be recognised by her family, and was involved in obscurity. It appeared that between the age of 49 and 50 she married a person named Jeremiah Smith, who was a Smith at Birmingham, by whom she had four children, and that she was afterwards married to a Mr. Bird. The Plaintiff's mother, Sarah King, was one of the four children by the first marriage, and lived to the age of 110 years. Elizabeth Jennens' birth was registered at Birmingham, on the 4th June, 1665 ; her first marriage on the 7th October, 1714; and her second, some time in 1733. The principal witnesses in support of the claim were the descendants of the four children by the first marriage. A pedigree and a religious book were submitted as additional evidence on behalf of the Plaintiff. This book had come into the possession of the Plaintiff directly from Elizabeth, in the year 1798—in which William Jennens died.

The following inscription was written on the inside of the cover of that book:—

"Elizabeth Jennings her book 15th June 1680 the gift of Humphrey Jennings her Father"

And on a blank leaf in the middle of the book were entries of the birth of the four children of Elizabeth.

For the Defendant it was contended that the inscriptions in the book were forgeries. In the first place the book itself was an abstruse and metaphysical disquisition, by Bishop Patrick, upon certain difficult theological doctrines, and could not, therefore, be supposed to have been placed by a father in the hands of a child of fourteen years of age for her spiritual edification. And next, the inscription was obviously not his handwriting, as it would be found on reference to his will, and that he spelt his name *Humfrey* Jennens, and the name in the book contained a "ph" in the first word and a "g" in the second. Neither could it have been written by the supposed Elizabeth; for a bond, executed near the date of her first marriage, conveyed her approbation and consent by a very substantial cross, which, in the opinion of Counsel, proves that Elizabeth was unable to write her own name; or, admitting that she might have signed it, was it probable that she could not spell the name of her own father?

Such was the argument urged by Counsel on behalf of the Defendant; and at the same time the wills of certain members of the family were produced in evidence to prove that no mention of Elizabeth was in any of them anywhere made. Had only Counsel examined those wills and contemporary documents, he would have discovered, as the writer has done, that in that age there was no uniformity in spelling; that "Humphrey" and "Humfrey" and "Jennens," "Jenens," "Jenyns," with several other phonetic styles, are frequently met with in the wills and documents; so that as to this one point his argument should fail.

As to Elizabeth's inability to write, no such theory was suggested as to the possibility of accident and temporary lameness at the time she signed the bond by making her cross.

As to the unfortunate Elizabeth being disowned by her wealthy relatives, under the circumstances, is nothing remarkable—such incidents happen every day. But in that time of infatuated intolerance and bitter persecution—when Royalist and Republican were alike opposed to Romanism—when anyone professing the old faith was subject to penal laws, which degraded our nation to a state of barbarism—when the Catholic and his friends were alike suspected and frequently accused and convicted of treason, and doomed to a horrible death—is it to be wondered at that Elizabeth's relatives, being rigorous Protestants, should have taken the course it is said they did, and treated her as an outcast? Further on will be given one of those instances of cruelty of that time, when people suffered miserable deaths on account of their religion.—(See Acton Place.)

Even admitting the hypothesis that Elizabeth was descended from Humphrey, her claim was too remote to entitle her to participate in the personalty of William Jennens' estate. For it will have been seen that the only persons rightly entitled are they who can prove their descent from John Jennens (No. 2), and not they who prove their descent from his brother Humphrey Jennens; the intestate, William Jennens, being the lineal descendant of John Jennens (No. 2).

But we are digressing.

The Vice-Chancellor, commenting on the case, said it would be impossible to say the Plaintiff had not made out such a case as at all events entitled her to an enquiry; but the great question for the consideration of the Court was whether the Elizabeth Jennens who was baptised on the 4th of January, 1665, and the description of the daughter of Humphrey Jennens was the person who married Jeremiah Smith in June, 1714. After giving his reasons for believing that Elizabeth pre-deceased her father, and without remarking upon the troublesome state of the times, he proceeded to comment on the inscriptions in the book. It was plain to him that the inscription on the inside of the cover of the book was not in the handwriting of the father or the children who signed the testamentary papers, and nothing could be more utterly unlikely than to suppose that a young lady educated in the manner in which each of Humphrey's children must have been educated should have made such a mistake as to write the name of her father with a " ph," when he uniformly was found using an " f." For that reason the memorandum must be supposed to have been written by some other person. Allusion was then made to the variety of families named Jennings living in and around Birmingham, and the theories of an educated lady having married a blacksmith; the change of religion and consequent persecution being rejected as extremely improbable. The Bill was dismissed with costs.

To resume, however, with the line of John (No. 2). We now proceed with Robert, the fourth child, who married Jane Truelock, at Aldworth Church, Berkshire, and had issue two children, namely, Martha and Robert. Martha died in infancy. Robert (the grandson of John No. 2) was born in 1672, and married Ann Guidott in 1700, and had issue one child only, namely, William, who was born and baptised in Middlesex in 1701, and died at Acton Place in Suffolk, a bachelor and intestate.

Roger, the fifth child of John (No. 2), married Isabel Rotherham, and had issue Jacob who married Ellen Mellor, and had issue William who married Martha Saunders, and had issue Jacob who married Betty Smith, and had issue Hannah and Martha. Hannah married John Harrison and had issue William and Thomas, who are now living. Martha married Daniel Willis and had issue Thomas and George.

Thomas Willis married Ruth Worrall and had issue four children,—Emma, Ann, Mary and Benjamin. Thomas Willis died in November, 1878.

George Willis married Ann Hinch, and is now living.

As soon as the members of the Jennens family who resided in Birmingham heard of the death of the late Wm. Jennens, they began to bestir themselves, and they became desirous to obtain proofs of their relationship. The Box containing the old Bible was sometime afterwards (about 1868) discovered and opened; but long before then there was an interchange of letters amongst the members of the family on the subject of their pedigree. To these letters, of which the following are copies, and particularly to those between Mrs. Anne Patrick, and Lady Andover and Mr. Richard Howard, the reader's attention is requested.

[COPY CORRESPONDENCE.]

" Birmingham Nov 28 98.

" Dear Sister and Brother

" I hope you will be kind enough to excuse the long silence it is not out of any disrespect far from it your kindness to us will never be erased from my mind, suppose you'll be suprised when I inform you that the late Mr. Jennens that died lately at Acton is a near relation of my mother's, and we are in hopes she will come in for all or part of the estate and personal property, we have had some trouble about it and find that the writings that were made by my mother's Grandfather John Jennens are in some hands in

Birmingham that won't give them up and we can do nothing without the Copy of the late Jennens grandfather's Will then we are in expectation of making it out to our advantage indeed I don't think there is a doubt about it. Now brother I have a favour to ask you that is to request you to go to Doctor's Common and ask the price of the Copy of Humphrey Jennens Will for we can do nothing without it. and send me word what the expense will be and how long it will be before we can have it down for the longer it is the greater trouble we shall have. My Grandfather was an eminent Ironmaster in Birmingham. Your Mother desires her love to you both and returns you thanks for your kind present. your sister joins us in their love to you so we must conclude.

    " Your affectionate Brother and Sister,
        " ISAAC AND ELIZ PERRY.

 "Please to direct for me in Hospital Street facing the Horse and Jockey.

" To Mr Joseph Perry
 " N° 11 Dene Street Soho
  " London"

       " Whitby, Decr 13th 1798.
" Dear Sir.

 " Some relations of the late James Essex by the name of Mary Blyth have made application to my Mother respecting some writings they apprehended were in her hands from which they expected to trace something that would lead very much to their advantage in the affairs of the late Mʳ Jennings if he had any she supposed they were put into your Father's hands and therefore desired them to apply to you as their prospect of success depends on the information to be gained from a sight of them she will consider it a favour done her by your putting them in some way as no doubt they are willing to make you a proper return, mother wishes in best respects to yourself and family.

" with Dear Sir Sincerely Yours,
" MARY HODGETTS.

" To Mʳ Higgins
" Birmingham "

" Birmingham Feb 18 99.
" Dʳ Brother and Sister
" We received your letter dated 16th and are much obliged to you for your kindness the reason we sent to you for your pedigree of the Jennens family was to know how near a relation John Jennens of Wednesbury Hall in the County of Stafford but last of Phillip Street in Birmingham was he was by trade a Bricklayer* if the Will of Humphrey Jennens does not give any accᵗ of him it must be in the Will of Humphrey's father but if he is not noticed in either of these Wills he certainly is in the pedigree it is the granddaughter

---

* That is, he had learnt the trade, although he was not under the necessity of following it. Most prudent parents then caused their children to be apprenticed to some trade, lest by the troublesome state of the times they should lose their possessions and become destitute.

F

of this man that is my mother she is now upwards of 80 years of age your further aplycation in this business will ever be considered as a grate faviour by your.

"This John Jennens has been dead upwards of 90 years.

"affectionate Brother & Sister
"I AND E. PERRY."

"To Mr Isaac Perry
"Hospital Street
"Facing The Horse and Jockey
"Birmingham.

"Dear Brother & Sister.

"According to your request I got an acquaintance of mine (a professional man) to apply to the Commons but find it is of no use as to the pedigree of the late Mr Jennings formerly of Acton. I understand the Will is there but that does not refer to any ancestors. You must therefore get me the names of some of his relations and I will immediately make the necessary inquiry of them and let you know the result thereof.

"I am your affectionate Brother & Sister
"JOSEPH AND ANN PERRY.

"N° 11 Dean Street Soho
"16th March 1799."

"Sir

"By your direction I got my friend to peruse your letter who assures me it is of no use to refer him to the

Will of either of the parties you mention, if you want the pedigree of any person under the Will of the late Mr Jennens of Acton in Middl^x it must be procured by the register of the different births and burials and which I understand must have been made in the County near where you now live.

" My friend says he is fearful you mistake a Copy of the Will for the pedigree if so you may have that at any time you please by writing me a line but I beg to inform you that the Copy of the Will will not at all inform you of the pedigree as that can only be procured by Certificates of the different Christenings, Deaths &c and which can only be got from the different Parish Churches wherein the same was taken.

" If I can offer this inquiry to be of any service I shall be happy to do it and remain Dr Brother and Sister

" Yrs affectionately

" JOSEPH AND ANN PERRY.

" 23rd March 1799."

" To Lady Mary Andover
" Elford Hall
" near Litchfield
" Staffordshire.

" Madam.

" I take the liberty of informing you that I have every reason to believe myself related at no great distance to the late William Jennens, Esqre of Acton deceased. My Great Grandfather by my mother's side was John Jennens Proprietor of Wednesbury Hall which he sold as will appear from the writings now in the hands of Lord Viscount Dudley and Ward the present possessors. My grandmother's name was Mary Jennens. She was the only child of the abovenamed John Jennens and was married from Dudston Hall to a Mr James Essex, of Dudston Mill. The issue of this marriage was two sons who died unmarried and two daughters Anne and Mary from the latter of whom I have the honour to be descended. Humphrey Jennens the Father of the late William had a Son of the name of John who might or might not be my Great Grandfather. I have not the presumption to say he was tho' many vain people would think so, particularly as the dates correspond. Your Ladyship being I make no doubt in possession of an accurate pedigree of the Family can easily determine the point. But tho' my ancestor might not be the son of Humphrey and brother of William I cannot help believing he was some near relation and I am induced to believe so far from a variety of concurring circumstances too long to be here specified. I beg pardon for thus intruding myself on Your Ladyship's notice and hope you will have ye goodness not to impute it to any improper motive in,

"Madam
"Your most obedient Servt
"ANNE PATRICK.

"Great Hampton Street
"Bir^m 16th May 1800."

Original Letter—one sheet of paper, bearing the postmark and date.

"To Mrs Patrick
"Great Hampton Street
"post paid Birmingham.

"Madam.

"I have to acknowledge the receipt of your letter dated 15th May 1800. to which I can make no other reply than to assure you that you are not in that Relationship to the late Mr Wm Jennens as your letter supposes.

"Your humble Servt
"M. ANDOVER.

"Elford. 22nd May 1800."

It is plain that Lady Andover takes advantage of the ignorance of Mrs. Anne Patrick. The latter has a vague idea that John Jennens (No. 1) was her ancestor, and that John Jennens (No. 2) was the uncle of William Jennens the intestate. Thus she imagines John (No. 2) to be identical with John, one of the sons of Humphrey Jennens, who was one of the brothers of John (No. 2).

The following sketch will illustrate Mrs. Anne Patrick's idea of the pedigree:—

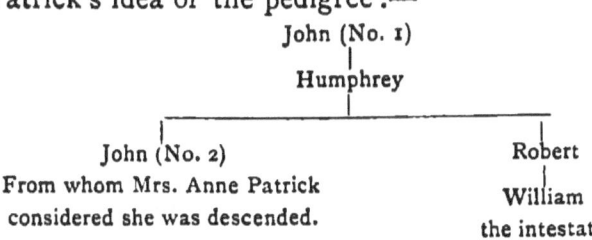

Now if this idea had been correct, she would have been equally entitled with Lady Andover and William Lygon, being in the same degree of relationship. Of course the mistake would be immediately detected; but it was seen that Mrs. Patrick in common with some others had also a mistaken idea of William's parentage, and advantage was taken of it accordingly. In fact Humphrey's descendants had no title to the property.

"Madam,

"Accept my thanks for your polite letter and permit me to apologize for once more intruding myself on your Ladyship's goodness. I have taken ye liberty of enclosing copies of the Wills of my Great Grandfather John Jennens and my Grandmother Mary Jennens afterwards Mary Essex his only child and I hope your Ladyship will see from a perusal of them that my pretensions to some degree of relationship to the late Mr William Jennens are not without some foundation. Your ladyship assures me "that I am not in that Relationship as my letter supposes" that I had not the presumption to say that John Jennens my Great Grandfather was the son of Humphrey and Uncle of William" I only flattered myself that he might stand in some degree of relationship or other but what I could not tell: and you will pardon me if I still think so, for upon the death of Mary Jennens my Grandmother, certain family Dresses came into my mother's possession which were so rich and splendid as to shew that my ancestors had once made a considerable figure in the world. There is a ridiculous Club in this Town endeavouring to make out among them some kind of title to the possessions of ye late Mr Wm Jennens but I assure you Madam I have had nothing to do either with them or their proceedings. I am far from claiming any part of that property. I write merely to gratify a curiosity excusable enough in the eyes of a person of your Ladyship's candour and Benevolence. If your Ladyship continues still convinced that I am in no way whatever related to the late Mr Wm Jennens it will be a great satisfaction to me and my family if you will have the goodness to assign your reason. I promise you Madam you shall not afterwards ever receive the least trouble from

"Madam
"Your most obed^t serv^t
"ANN PATRICK.

" To Lady Andover
" June 3—1800."

Original letter with post mark and date.
" To Mrs Patrick
" Great Hampton Street
" Birmingham
" post paid

" Madam,
"I am sorry that you mistook that expression is my letter of the 5th of the last month concerning my mentioning your relationship to the late Mr Jennens, my words were these, viz. *I can make no reply than to*

assure you that you are not in that relationship to Mr Jennens as your letter supposes. I suppose all the Jennens family were in some degree related to him as well as Mr Lygon and *myself.* who am the last living of all my Mothers children. I return you the Wills you sent me and beg leave to inform you that Richd Howard Esqre my Son in Law has full powers from me to administer for me in all business relating to the late Mr Jennen's Fortune. to him I refer you who I dare say will take care that you are lawfully convinced of all our proceedings on your immediate application to him.

[The direction is to Richard Howard, Esq., Lower Brook Street, Grosvenor Square, London.]
"This is all Madam that I can reply to you.
" Your humble serv^t
" M. ANDOVER."

" Madam,
"Lady Andover having informed me that you are anxious to learn in what degree of relationship you stand to the late Mr Wm Jennens and that you had sent to her certain family Wills which you thought might throw a light on the subject (but which she returned to you.) I have to say that if it should be agreeable to you to send Copies of them to me I will endeavour to collect from them the instructions necessary to satisfie your curiosity; for in respect of benefit none can arise from being related to Mr Jennens except to those who were living and in the same degree

as Lady Andover and Mr Lygon. They only were next akin, surviving at the time of Mr Jennens death.

"I am Madam
"Your humble Servt
"R. HOWARD.

"Brook Street
"June 7. 1800.
"To Mrs Anne Patrick
"at
"Birmingham."

The above is a copy of the original letter, which bears the post mark and mark.

At the foot of the letter is a memorandum in pencil, as follows:—

"My grandmother lived one year after the death of Wm Jennens Esq.

"J. P."

[COPY.]

"To Mr R. Howard
"From Mrs Patrick

"Sir.

"Agreeably to your polite request and my promise I enclosed Copies of the Wills of my Great Grandfather John Jennens and my Grandmother Mary Jennens afterwards Mary Essex his only child. The above John Jennens was Proprietor of Wednesbury Hall which he sold and his daughter Mary my Grandmother was married from Dudston Hall to a Mr James Essex of Dudston Mill. The issue of this marriage was two sons who died unmarried and two daughters Anne who is dead having left three daughters Mary—Elizabeth—and Anne. and Mary my mother who died last June. aged 86 and who left living besides myself one son Thomas and two daughters Elizabeth and Hannah. Humphrey Jennens ye grandfather of the late William had a son of ye name of John but as I told Lady Andover I have not the presumption to suppose my ancestor was that identical John nor have I any expectation that our family is in such degree of relationship to ye late William Jennens as will entitle us to any part of his property. I never entertained an idea of that kind but as a notion of some sort of relationship has prevailed in our family and as it is evident from certain rich and superb dresses formerly in ye possession of my mother that her ancestors once made a considerable figure in life I wish to be completely satisfied on the subject. I therefore shall be much obliged to you if you will point out whether or not we are, and in what degree related to. ye late William Jennens and if it is not too much trouble to assign your reasons it will gratify an innocent curiosity and be considered as a favour by

"Sir,

"June 30. 1800."   "Your very obed^t Servt

Addressed to Richard Howard, Esq., Brook Street, Grosvenor Square, London.

Original letter from R. Howard to Mrs. Patrick, bears post mark and date :—

" Madam.

" Absence from home and other circumstances have prevented me from sooner acknowledging your letter (with the Wills) of the 30th June. Neither the Wills nor any papers in my possession enable me to determine whether you stand in any or what degree of relationship to the late Mr Jennens. That you are not one of the next of kin is evident and indeed I need not repeat this opinion as you appear yourself to be perfectly satisfied on that point. The Jennens were I believe very numerous in the neighbourhood of Birmingham. If I should hereafter trace your connection with the person in question I shall be happy to inform you.

" I am Madam
" Your obe^t humble Servt
" R. HOWARD.

" Ashtead Park
" July 12th 1800."

Addressed to Mrs. Anne Patrick, Birmingham.

Original letter, with post mark and date, addressed as follows :—

" Epsom Oct 9th 1800.
" Mrs Anne Patrick
" Birmingham.

" Madam.

" I am rather surprised you should persist in requiring from Lady Andover particulars relative to your family which she has already declared herself unable to give. For my own part I have nothing to say on the subject which is not expressed in my former letters. I did not return the Wills (of which I concluded you had duplicates) to save the expense of Postage. I now make use of an opportunity of sending them free from that charge and am Madam.

"Your obedient humble Servt
"R. Howard.

"Ashtead Park
  "Octr 9 1800.

All the letters purporting to be written and signed by the lady representing herself to be Lady Andover, as also those purporting to be written and signed by Mr. Richard Howard, her son-in-law, are evidently written by one and the same person. Judging from the difference in style between these letters, and the Will and Codicil of Lady Andover, hereinafter referred to, it is also evident that her "Ladyship" occasionally wrote herself, and sometimes employed an amanuensis.

John (No. 2) was the father of John (No. 3), who was the father of Mary Essex, who was the mother of Mary Blyth, who was the mother of Anne Patrick, who was sister to Thomas Blyth, from whom James Baylis is descended, and also sister to Elizabeth Perry, from whom the Rhodes families are descended.

John Jennens (No. 2) was living in Reading, in Berkshire, from 1630 to 1641. He was apprenticed to a linen draper at Reading, served his time there, and married Jane Ambrose, at East Garston Church, in 1636. From 1630 to 1641 he was paying taxes at Reading. Man's History of Reading, p. 323, refers to John Jennens purchasing a piece of land, and his gift of the same to the above-mentioned Church to enlarge the Burial Ground. John Jennens and Jane (formerly Ambrose) had issue as follows: Jane 1637, John (No. 3) 1640, William 1643, Robert 1644, and Roger 1653. Robert and Roger were born at Duffield, in Derbyshire, to which place John and Jane had gone to live, either from Birmingham, in consequence of a dispute with Humphrey, John's half-brother, respecting some property belonging to their father at Shotwell (Shottle) and Duffield, in Derbyshire, or from London, to escape his political enemies. There are two versions of the case.

There is no trace of this John and Jane in Berkshire after 1641; but in the year 1642 he is found in business connections with John (No. 1), and is in an Agreement under seal, to which his father and himself were parties, described as John Jennens the younger, of Birmingham, juxta Aston; and in the same year, in another deed, he agrees to manage a business beforetime conducted by Ambrose, his uncle, in London, on behalf of his father and Esther, the widow of his late uncle Ambrose, deceased. On the commencement of the Civil War in 1642, John (No. 2) suddenly left London, and retired to Mobourne Mill, as previously stated. Soon afterwards it was reported he was dead, and in the suit "Jennens v. Norton" John (No. 1) seeks to obtain from Norton, the alleged administrator, an account of certain effects belonging to the estate of his "late" son John. By his father and his brother Humphrey he seems to have been considered as dead. It is more than probable that John (No. 2) was a political offender—perhaps a fugitive to save his life: it might have been a friendly act to assume that he was dead, and letters of administration would be granted to a creditor after a reasonable time, as in the case of Roger Norton, on the supposition of his death. If anyone can produce a certificate of his death before 1673, there will be an end of this theory. If, however, it should be proved that John (No. 2) predeceased his father, and so shew the impossibility of his having a son Roger, there will still be the descendants of John (No. 3), and as their claim has never yet been brought before the Court so as to be investigated, but was dismissed with costs by the tacit consent of the Counsel on both sides, there is yet hope that with the additional proofs which since then have been obtained, that the case may be tested on its merits.

After the supposed death of John (No. 2), Robert his son returned to Berkshire and married Jane Truelock, at Aldworth Church, and had issue two children,— Martha, who died in infancy, and Robert, who married Anne Guidott, and had issue William of Acton the intestate.

Robert the son of John (No. 2) when an infant of five years of age was entered at the Middle Temple.

This seems to have been then the custom. He died when his son Robert was only 11 years old. (See Mrs. Somerton's Affidavit.)

Robert was then sent to live with his uncle Edward Jennens, of the Middle Temple, London.

As a further proof of Mrs. Somerton's statement being correct, there is the application for the marriage licence of Robert Jennings and Anne Guidott.

Robert was born in 1644, consequently when he died in 1683 he was 39 years old. His son Robert was born in 1672, and when his father died he was 11 years old. Seventeen years afterwards, in 1700, an application is made for the marriage licence, and in this he is described as being of the age of 28 years.

The following is a copy of the application referred to:

16th Octr 1700.

." Which day appeared personally John Evans of the parish of St. Andrew Holborn in the County of Middlesex aged fourty years Merchant and alleged that there is a marriage intended to be solemnized between Robert Jennings of the Middle Temple London aged 28 years and a bachelor and Ann Guidott of the Parish of St. Andrew Holborne aforesaid aged above 21 years and a Spinster with the consent of Carew Guidott Father to the said Ann he not knowing nor believing any impediment by reason of any precontract consanguinaty affinity or any other lawful means whatsoever to hinder the said intended marriage of ye truth of which he made Oath and prayed Licence for them to be married in y^e

Parish Church of St. Giles in the Fields in the County of Middlesex.

"Jurat   "JOHN EVANS.
  "T. Cooke
    "Surr."

The Licence was granted, and the marriage took place in Westminster Abbey the same year. In the following year their son William of Acton was born, and he was baptised at St. Giles-Church-in-the-Fields, King William the Third being one of the sponsors.

When William was only 7 years of age his father bought Acton Place, in the parish of Acton, in the County of Suffolk, of the then owner John Daniel.

The name of Acton, together with that of its owner, reminds one of those fearful times of intolerance and persecution to which reference has been made in the suit Hood *v.* Beauchamp. It was then stated that Elizabeth, one of the daughters of Humphrey Jennens, became a Roman Catholic, and married a man of inferior position to herself; in consequence of which she was disowned by her family and by them was treated as an outcast. The Vice-Chancellor could not believe her family to be capable of such cruelty, and appeared to be oblivious of the fierce persecution which then prevailed. The following short account from Dr. Challoner's work will give an idea of what really was the case:—

"One Arthur Bell was born of both virtuous and good families, his father having a seat at Temple

ACTON PLACE.

Broughton, in the parish of Hanbury, about 6 miles from Worcester, and his mother being the sister to Francis Daniel, Esq., of Acton Place, near Long Melford, in Suffolk. At the age of 24 he left Acton Place, where for some years he had been living with his uncle, and went over to the English College of St. Alban the Martyr in Valladolid. Having completed his studies he returned to England in Sepr., 1643. The Civil War commenced the previous year. On the 6th Novr. in that year he was apprehended as a spy by some Soldiers of the Parliament, who at first treated him as a spy, but on discovering that he was a Catholic Priest they took him before the Committee then sitting in Hertfordshire, to whom all the papers which had been found upon him were delivered. He was tried on the 7th of Decr. following, and being convicted of being a Catholic Priest (and nothing more) he was condemned to die, and on the 11th of the same month he was brought out of Newgate and placed on a hurdle which was drawn by four horses to Tyburn, where he was cruelly killed according to the barbarous custom of the time, being for a short time only hanged by the neck and then allowed to revive, and whilst yet living his belly ripped open and his bowels torn out and burnt in a large fire prepared for that purpose before his face. He was then quartered and his members were exhibited to the public gaze as those of a traitor." Yet by conforming to the then existing law and renouncing his priesthood he could have saved his life.

G

Happily there is no likelihood of a recurrence of such horrors. The working class are now politically invincible, and can and would prevent them; and they can if so disposed legislate almost as they please. There is no statute which may not be repealed, no custom but may not be discontinued, if they become oppressive to the poor. Let the people be but loyal and true to themselves; let them send to Parliament men of honest principle, and very soon there would be such a moral change in England as would leave little reason for anyone to complain.

With the aid of such men, the Ministry have become the representative and the executive of the people, and practically we are more republican in our government than any other nation.

The following is a copy of the commencement of one of two Indentures, being the conveyance of Acton Place to Humphrey Jennens, of Erdington, in the County of Warwick, Esq., and Anthony Guidott, of Lincoln's Inn, in the County of Middlesex, Gentleman. The premises were conveyed to them in trust for Robert Jennens, the father of William Jennens the intestate. It will be seen that in one of the deeds there is a Robert Jennens of Ardington mentioned. It is believed that this Robert Jennens is the son of Humphrey Jennens, and not Robert Jennens the grandson of John (No. 2) and the father of the intestate :—

" This deed made the eight and twentieth day of December in the 7th year of the reign of our sovereign Lady Ann by the grace of God Queen of Great Brittaine

France and Ireland Defender of the Faith &c Anno Domi 1708. Between John Daniell of Acton Place in the Parish of Acton in the County of Suffolk Esqr son and heire of Charles Daniell late of Overhall in the County of Essex Esq. deceased who was son and heire of John Daniell late of Acton in the said County of Suffolk Esqr also deceased of the one part and Humphrey Jennens* of Ardington in the County of Warwick Esqr and Anthony Guidott of Lincoln's Inn in the County of Middlesex Gentleman of the other part. Witnesseth that for and in consideration of the sum of £12700 of good and lawful money of Great Brittaine to the said John Daniell party hereto in hand well and truely paid by the said Humphrey Jennens and Anthony Guidott att and before the ensealing and delivery of these presents for the absolute purchase of the mannors messuages farms lands tenements and hereditaments hereinafter particularly described being the same sume of £12700 mentioned to be the consideration of certain Indentures of 13 parts bearing even date with these presents and made between the said John Daniell party to these presents of the first part. The Most Noble John Duke of Marlborough Knight of the *most* order of the Garter of the second part. William Guidott of Lincoln's Inn in the Coy. of Middlesex Esqr sole executor of the last Will and Testament of Anthony Guidott late of Lincoln's Inn aforesaid gentlemen deceased and George Golden of Newhouse in the Parish

---

* This is Humphrey the son of Humphrey, and a cousin of Robert the father of William once removed.

of Poslingford in the said County of Suffolk Esq. of the third part. May Daniell of Acton Place in the County of Suffolk Widow and Relict of the said Charles Daniell and alsoe Administratrix of the goods and chattells of Anne Daniell one of her daughters by the said Chas Daniell of the fourth part. *Robert Jennens of Ardington aforesaid Esq.* of the fifth part. Thomas Stisted of Ipswich in the County of Suffolk Genlemen John Morley of Halstead in the County of Essex Gentlemen and Isaac Hobart of Stoke juxta Clare in the said County of Suffolk Gentleman of the sixth part. Richard Gipps of London Esqr of the seventh part. Patrick Lacy of the Inner Temple London Esqr of the eighth part. Thomas Unwin of London Grocer of the ninth part. Thomas Fowler of London Grocer of the tenth part. The said Humphrey Jennens and Anthony Guidott party to these presents of the eleventh part. Oliver Martin of the Middle Temple London gentlemen and Christopher Widmore of Lincoln's Inn aforesaid gentleman of the twelfth part and William Jennens[*] of Ardington aforesaid Esq. and Peter Froude of Grayes Inn in the County of Middlesex Esq. of the thirteenth part purporting to be a grant and release of the said mannors, messuages farmes lands tenements and hereditaments from the said John Duke of Marlborough, *Robert Jennens*, Thomas Stisted, John Morley, Isaac Hobart, and John Daniell party to these presents to the said Humphrey Jennens and Anthony Guidott party to these presents and their heires &c"

---

[*] Son of Humphrey Jennens.

" The claimants contend that Robert Jennens, of Bedford Row, Holborn, the actual purchaser, cannot be identical with Robert Jennens of Ardington, one of the conveying parties, and they submit this point for the consideration of the reader. The papers disclose nothing further as to this. Having purchased Acton Place, Robert Jennens began to erect a noble mansion, which he was on the point of completing when he died suddenly of apoplexy.* It is said to have been a most noble and magnificent country seat, which for the grandeur of its hall and the massive elegance of its marble chimney-pieces, as well as the beauty and extent of its stables and other offices, was totally unrivalled in that part of the county. The staircase, however, and one entire wing of the house, which was to have been principally to a vast and superb ball-room, were left totally incomplete; and notwithstanding the son when he attained his majority found himself possessed of real and personal estate of not less than £200,000, he never added another stroke to the unfinished structure, which remained in precisely the same state in which it was left on the decease of its more worthy projector. In this extensive palace, for it scarcely deserves a meaner appellation, Mr. Jennings resided when in the country to the latest hour of his life—yet not in the finished and family apartments, but merely in the basement floor alone, which by being not less than 10 or 15 feet below the surface of the court, and

* From Notes to the Pedigree, British Museum, add MS. 19137, for 173.

illuminated by small and heavy windows, admitted but very seldom the reviving rays of the sun in any direction. Here on a level with most of the offices of this superb pile of building, in the midst of his servants, was his breakfast room, his dining room and his bed chamber, the entire furniture of which was of his own procuring and consequently very mean, and its whole value perhaps did not exceed £20; nor were the rooms above (excepting those in the wing already described), although completely and magnificently furnished by his father, ever opened but once during the whole period of his possessing them, which extended to near a century. He had nevertheless more family pride than Mr. Elwes, and maintained a table in some degree superior. In this dark and miserable compartment of the house his dinner was always served up, even when he was alone, (and he was seldom otherwise) in the family plate, nor if any portion remained after the wants of his diminutive household had been satisfied, would he suffer it to be again introduced to assist in the dinner of the ensuing day. The poor, however, were never benefitted by this profusion of diet, for it was his express order, and an order uniformly adhered to, that the surplus should be distributed amongst his dogs. He was never known throughout the whole period of his life to exhibit one single charitable action; and so cold and unsocial was his animal constitution that a male friend was never invited to sleep beneath his roof, and there is no instance of a female of any description having been indebted to him for the hospitality of a single night. In these respects he was a character infinitely more despicable than his neighbour, who at all times evinced the utmost degree of politeness and gallantry to the fair sex, and who, if he withheld his hand from the needy, withheld it in an equal degree from himself. In his mode of increasing his property Mr. Jennings was also a more contemptible miser. Elwes when in London occasionally frequented the gaming table; but it was to participate with his associates in the various chances of the dice. Jennings too frequented it, and was in reality at one period of his life an habitual attendant at Brooke's or White's; but it was not to partake in the multiplied fortunes of gaming, but to accommodate the unlucky with money for the evening, and to draw an enormous profit from the general loss. It is asserted that for every £1000 he thus advanced he received the next morning 1000 guineas. To enable him to persevere steadily in this profitable concern, he ventured to purchase a house in Grosvenor Square, where indeed he occasionally resided to the day of his death, a long time, after the infirmities of age compelled him to relinquish his dishonourable traffic. On quitting either his town or his country house he was accustomed to draw up with his own hand an inventory of articles left behind, even to the minutest and most insignificant, and to examine them with the most rigid scrutiny on his return, to satisfy himself that he had not been wronged of his property. The arrangement of this catalogue when he was quitting the country was attended with no small degree of labour; for, according to the fashion of our forefathers, almost all the chimney-pieces throughout the house had been left to him furnished with an infinite variety of pieces of china, small as well as large. Every little dog and duck, however, every teacup, ewer and other toy, was duly noticed, and expected to be found on his return, not only uninjured but accurately occupying its immediate post."

"To diminish the expenses paid to his housekeeper (or rather an old woman who kept his house), he used to allow it to be seen by strangers, and, like a noble Duke and Duchess of the present day [meaning the time when the MS. was written], to permit her to add to her wages the gratuities offered on such occasions. The bargain being thus mutually acceded to, the house was equally open for inspection whether he were in it or not; and, in the former case, when the company had reached the subterranean floor where he constantly resided, he removed from room to room till the whole had been visited. He had but a small circle of acquaintance in the country; he did not like however to be totally without occasional company, and induced some few gentlemen to pay him morning visits and to profess considerable friendship for him, by the promise of legacies in his will. And, so far indeed as related to the literal promise itself, he punctually fulfilled it; for he not only made his Will but bequeathed the expected legacies; yet he took effectual care at the same time that neither his promises nor his will should possess much validity, for he never executed the latter, *and his entire property at his death, amounting to a little less than a million sterling, was in the first instance likely to become the subject of a* CHANCERY SUIT BETWEEN TWO NOBLE FAMILIES, *who advanceed an equal claim of* HEIRSHIP. *This suit however was shortly afterwards dropped upon an agreement between the parties to* DIVIDE *the property in tranquility.* The only creditable trait in the character of this miser is, that he never oppressed his tenants. He would never advance them a shilling for their accommodation, but he never raised their rents nor distressed them for want of punctuality in their payments; and yet, while he thus rigidly forebore from every act of kindness and charity, he was for the last 20 years previous to his death losing upwards of £2000 annually by the large sums of money he retained unemployed in the hands of his bankers. He kept cash at two separate houses; and it was discovered at his death that in one of them he had never possessed less than £20,000 for the last 20 years previous, and in the other he had uniformly had a large sum for a longer period. He died in the year 1797-8, in the 97th year of his age." (Eccentric Mirror, Vol. 1, p. 26).

This miser was the last survivor in a Tontine established in the reign of William the Third, his royal godfather. From this Tontine he received for some years an annuity of £1000. His last Will under the description of "William Jennens, Esq., of Bedford Row," is dated May 3rd 1726, a few weeks after his father's sudden death.

The following is a copy of the Will:—

" In the name of God amen I William Jennens of

of sound and disposing mind memory and understanding make this my last Will and Testament in manner following Impris: I will that all my just debts shall be paid and satisfied. Item. I give and devise unto my honoured mother Anne Jennens all those my estates in the several Counties of Suffolk and Essex which were purchased by my late Father of John Daniel for the sum of Twelve thousand seven hundred pounds in the names of *Humphrey Jennens and Anthony Guidott Trustees for my said late Father. And also all other my estates whatsoever in said Counties of Suffolk and Essex with their and every of their appurtenances. To hold to my said mother during the term of her natural life May 3rd 1726.

"WILLIAM JENNENS.

"Signed sealed published and declared by the said Testator William Jennens as and for his last Will and Testament in the presence of us who have subscribed our names as Witnesses. Edmund Harris—Elizabeth Harris—William Snell."

William Jennens duly took out Letters of Administration on the death of his father. The following is the office copy extract from the principal Registry of Her Majesty's Court of Probate :—

"In the Prerogative Court of Canterbury
"Martii 1726.

"Robertus Jennens decimo sexto die emt Com^o Gulielmo Jennens ar. filio urale et ltimo et unicæ Proli Roberti Jennens nuper parochiæ St Andræ Holborn in

---
* Testator does not describe this Humphrey as his uncle.

Com. Middxiæ. Ar defti heutis &c. ad administrandum bona jurà et credita dicti defuncti de bene &c. Jurat."

Admon of goods unadministered, passed in June, 1803.

On the death of his mother, Anne Jennens, her son William Jennens also took out Letters of Administration. The following is a copy extract:—

"In the Prerogative Court of Canterbury

"March 1762.

"Ann Jennens. On the tenth day administration of the goods chattels and credits of Ann Jennens late of the Parish of St. George Hanover Square in the County of Middlesex Widow deceased was granted to William Jennens Esq. the natural and lawful son of the said deceased having been first sworn duly to administer."

Admon of goods unadministered in July, 1798.

From the two foregoing documents it is evident that Robert Jennens predeceased his wife, and that Ann Jennens predeceased her son. How then came William Lygon in 1803 to describe the said Robert Jennens as a widower? If the present be the original inscription on the tomb in Acton Church, had he not an opportunity to read it (and if it be true) to correctly describe the deceased? The inference is, the present inscription is not the original one, and as he had no real proof of the identity of the deceased, he described him as a widower, believing him to have been the fourth son of Humphrey Jennens. Now Robert Jennens, of

Erdington, the fourth son of Humphrey Jennens, was a widower.

The following is the copy extract from the Court of Probate.

"In the Prerogative Court of Canterbury
"June 1803.

"Robert Jennens Esqr. On the second day administration of the Goods Chattels and Credits of Robert Jennens late of the Parish of Saint Andrew Holborn in the County of Middlesex Esquire *Widower*. deceased left unadministered by William Jennens Esquire the natural and lawful son only child and *sole person* entitled to the personal estate and effects of the said deceased since also deceased was granted to William Lygon Esq the surviving administrator (with the Will annexed of the goods of the said William Jennens) he having been first sworn to administer. Effects under £20. Former Grant March 1726."

The question is, did William Lygon act wilfully or in error? If he had been well acquainted with the history of William Jennens he would not have described his father Robert Jennens as a widower, for he could easily have learned by reading the inscription on the Acton monument (supposing it to have been then as it now appears) that Robert Jennens died before his wife, and that consequently his widow was entitled to participate in the estate along with her only child William Jennens under the Statute of Distributions.

Further comment hereon will become necessary.

At Stoke juxta Clare, at a short distance from Acton Place, resided Sir Harvey Elwes, the intimate acquaintance of William Jennens. These two monomaniacs would sit for hours together devising some selfish and ungodly mode of thrift. It is said that one evening Elwes called upon Jennens and surprised him as he was indulging himself with the dim light of a tallow candle. Elwes sat down and introduced the favourite subject of economy; whereupon Jennens immediately blew out the candle, observing that they could just as well discuss that subject in the dark. Shobert, in his "Beauties of England," when treating of Stoke juxta Clare devotes considerable space to the eccentricities of Elwes. He says—

"In the annals of avarice there is not a more celebrated name than that of Elwes. The accumulation of money was the only passion and employment of the long life of Sir Hervey, who though given over in his youth for a consumption, attained to the age of upwards of eighty years. To avoid the expense of company, he doomed himself for upwards of sixty years to the strictest solitude, scarcely knew the indulgence of fire or candle, and resided in a mansion where the wind entered at every broken casement and the rain descended through the roof. His household consisted of one man and two maids, and such was the systematic economy which governed the whole establishment that the annual expenditure of Sir Hervey, though worth at least £250,000, amounted to £110. Amongst the few acquaintances he had, says Mr. Topham, was an occasional club at his own village of Stoke, and there were members of it two Baronets besides himself—Sir Cordwell Firebras and Sir John Bernardiston. However rich they were, the reckoning was always an object of their investigation. As they were one day settling this difficult point, an oddfellow, who was a member, called out to a friend who was passing, 'For heaven's sake step up stairs, and assist the poor! Here are three Baronets, worth a million of money, quarrelling about a farthing!' On the death of Sir Hervey, in 1763, he lay in state, such as it was, at Stoke; and some of his tenants observed with more humour than decency that it was well he could not see it. His immense property devolved to his nephew, John Meggott, who by his will was ordered to assume the name and arms of Elwes.

"Mr. Elwes (whose mother had been left a widow by a rich brewer, with a fortune of £100,000, and starved herself to death), proved himself a worthy heir to her and Sir Hervey. On his first coming to Stoke, after his uncle's death, he began, it is true, to keep fox hounds; and his stable of hunters at that time was said to be the best in the kingdom. This was the only instance in the whole life of Mr. Elwes of his sacrificing money to pleasure; but even here everything was conducted in so frugal a manner that the whole of his establishment—huntsmen, dogs and horses—did not cost him £300 a year. After a residence of near 14 years at Stoke, he was chosen to represent Berkshire in Parliament: on which occasion he removed to his seat at Marcham, in that county. He now relinquished the keeping of horses and dogs, and no man could be more attentive to his senatorial duties than Mr. Elwes while he continued to sit in the House of Commons. On his retirement from public life, to avoid the expense of a contested election, he was desirous of visiting his seat at Stoke, where he had not been for some years. When he reached this place, once the seat of more active scenes of somewhat resembling hospitality, and where his fox hounds had diffused something like vivacity around, he remarked that 'he had formerly expended a great deal of money very foolishly, but that a man grows wiser in time.'"

Of the way of living of this accomplished miser during this, his last residence at Stoke, the following account is given by his biographer:—

"The rooms at his seat at Stoke—that were now much out of repair and would have all fallen in but for his son John Elwes, Esq., who had resided there—he thought too expensively furnished, as worse things might have done. If a window was broken there was to be no repair but that of a little brown paper or piecing in a bit of broken glass, which had at length been done so frequently and in so many shapes that it would have puzzled a mathematician to say what figure they described. To save fire he would walk about the remains of an old greenhouse, or sit with a servant in the kitchen. During the harvest he would amuse himself by going into the fields to glean the corn on the grounds of his own tenants; and they used to leave a little more than common to please the old gentleman,

who was as eager after it as any pauper in the parish. In the advance of the season his morning employment was to pick up any stray chips, bones and other things to carry to the fire, in his pocket, and he was one day surprised by a neighbouring gentleman in the act of pulling down a crow's nest for that purpose. On the gentleman wondering why he gave himself this trouble —'Oh! Sir,' replied old Elwes, 'it is really a shame that these creatures should do so: do but see what waste they make! They don't care how extravagant they are.' As no gleam of favourite passion or any ray of amusement broke through this gloom of penury, his insatiable desire of saving was now become uniform and systematic. He used still to ride about the country on one of the worn out mares; but then he rode her very economically on the soft turf adjoining the road, without putting himself to the expense of shoes, as, he observed, "the turf was so pleasant to a horse's foot." When any gentleman called to pay him a visit and the boy who attended in the stable was profuse enough to put a little hay before the horse, old Elwes would slily steal back and take it carefully away. That very strong appetite which Mr. Elwes had in some measure restrained during the long sitting of Parliament he now indulged most voraciously, and on everything he could find. To save as he thought the expense of going to a butcher, he would have a whole sheep killed, and so eat mutton
sic
to the end of the chapter. When he occasionally had his river drawn, though sometimes horse loads of small fish were taken, not one would he suffer to be thrown

in again, for he observed 'he should never see them again.' Game in the last stage of putrefaction and meat that walked about his plate would he continue to eat rather than have new things killed before the old provision was finished. With this diet, the charnel house of sustenance, his dress kept pace, equally in the last stage of dissolution. Sometimes he would walk about in a tattered brown coloured morning gown and sometimes in a red and white woollen cap, like a prisoner confined for debt. His shoes he never would suffer to be cleaned, lest they should be worn out the sooner. When any friends who might occasionally be with him were absent, he would carefully put out his own fire, walk to the house of a neighbour, and thus make one fire serve for both. But still with all this self-denial—this penury of life to which the inhabitant of an almshouse is not doomed—still did he think himself profuse, and frequently say 'he must be a little more careful of his property.'

"The scene of mortification at which Mr. Elwes had now arrived was all but a denial of the common necessaries of life, and indeed it might have admitted a doubt whether, if his manors, his fish ponds and some grounds in his own hands had not furnished a subsistence where he had not anything actually to buy, he would not rather have starved than have bought anything. He one day during this period dined upon the remaining part of a moor hen which had been brought out of the river by a rat, and at another ate the undigested part of a pike which a larger one had swallowed but had not finished, and which were taken in this state in a net. At the time this last circumstance happened, he discovered a strange kind of satisfaction, observing, 'Aye, this was killing two birds with one stone.' In the room of all comment let it be remarked that at this time Mr. Elwes was perhaps worth near £800,000."

"This extraordinary man died November 26th, 1789, at his seat at Marcham, in Berkshire, having by will bequeathed all his real and personal estate, to the value of half a million sterling, to his two natural sons, George and John Elwes, who at the time this memoir was written (1813) were the proprietors of Stoke."

The following are extracts from Davy's Suffolk Collections, copied from the MS. in the British Museum :—

"Robert Jennens, Esq., the father of William, died in 1725. He purchased Acton Place Estate (about 200 acres only) of a Mr. Daniel, whose family had resided there several hundred years.—(Mag. Brit. p. 326.) He began to build the house, but died before he could have finished it, and it does not appear notwithstanding his son's immense wealth, that much if anything had been done towards its completion after his death; for, though a noble mansion, sixteen rooms of it were never completely finished. In explanation of this remark, I beg to add that on my minutely inspecting the exterior of the structure some months back, for the purpose of ascertaining the period of its erection, I discovered in the brickwork near the top of one of the chimneys the figures 1725—the very year in which the founder died, so that the shell or skeleton, at least, must have been erected in his lifetime. But the period of its erection is, however, of no consequence; and yet it is, for what seems trifling and insufficient to the majority of the community—if I may so express myself—is interesting and important to the antiquarians. Besides this, the short duration of Acton Place mansion, now in ruins, having scarcely stood a century, shows the vanity of all human greatness. This noble structure, whose tempting aspect had in vain drawn many a traveller from his road, had fifty-four apartments, of which not a vestige now remains, having been taken down this year by order of Earl Howe, heir-at-law of the late parsimonious proprietor."

Thomas Cromwell in his "Excursions through Suffolk in 1818," vol. I, p. 55, describes Acton Place as follows:—

"Acton Place was formerly the seat of the Daniels, but sold by them to Robert Jennens, Esq., who began to rebuild this mansion, which, though a fine structure, was never completely finished. His son, William Jennens, Esq., died in 1791, at the age of 93—some say at 100—with the reputation of being at that time the richest subject in the kingdom. On his decease the fine tapestry was torn from the walls, and sold with the furniture and other moveables. This noble mansion, having since that time been inhabited only by an old man and a woman, presented a deplorable spectacle of desolation, and the approach to it could be traced only by the colour and height of the grass, which had grown over the gravel. The interior still exhibited some vestiges of its former splendour. The hall is adorned with alto relievos, and the ceiling with the paintings from the heathen mythology. At each corner was also a figure of one of the fabled divinities. At the end and on each side were paintings of fruit and animals by Lynders. Some circular recesses also contained six busts, of admirable workmanship. In the panels over the fireplaces were *portraits of the late proprietor and his parents* ;* and the library contained a beautiful fruit-piece by Lynders. A curious specimen of female industry of former days was also exhibited here, in what was denominated the paint room, the whole of which was hung with needlework in blue and white, the furniture of the bed and chairs being the same. The adjoining apartment was called the silk room, from the elegant-painted silk with which it was furnished. Another curiosity exhibited here was a small bed, the furniture of which was said to have been lined with the shirts of King William the Third, who had been godfather to one of the owners of this mansion. The offices, forming wings on each side of the house, gives the whole the appearance of grandeur. The garden fared worse than the building, having been ploughed up and cultivated as a field. This property on the death of Mr. Jennens descended to the Hon. Penn Asheton Curzon."

Acton Place is still a gentleman's country seat, but really it only consists of the brewhouse and bakehouse

---

* Some of these have been traced; perhaps the intent was to destroy them and with them everything which might prove his paternity. The present owner is favourable to the Claimants.

ACTON PLACE.

which formed one of the wings of the former palatial mansion. Judging from the appearance of the present dwelling house, one can but vaguely imagine the beauty and grandeur of Acton Place as it once was; and its destruction is to be condemned as an act of Vandalism. Probably there was a motive for removing every trace which might have led to the discovery of the parentage of the late Wm. Jennings. The portraits of his parents adorned the mantelpieces, and there might possibly be concealed in some part of the mansion a recess containing documents of great value to his poor relations. Having obtained the property by certain means (which for the last 80 years have been deemed to be unlawful), it was of course prudential on the owners' part to avoid the risk of discovery, and consequently the place was dismantled and the materials were sold by public auction. The said Robert Jennens the father of William died suddenly in London, and was buried in Acton Church. The following is extracted from Davy's Suffolk Collections, MS. 19077, fo. 52, in the British Museum, being Church notes taken Augt. 18th, 1826:—

"The Church consists of a chancel, nave and aisles, and a Chapel at the East end of the South aisle. The Chancel is 20 feet 8 inches long and 15 feet 6 inches wide, covered with tiles and boards painted blue; the Communion Table is raised one step, boarded and railed off with a neat bannister; the East end wainscotted. In the East windows are three pieces of modern painted glass without meaning. On the sides of the windows are two tablets: that on the North side had the Lord's Prayer and Belief; that on the South, the Commandments.

The Chancel is open to the North aisle by the Monument No. 1 thereinafter described, to the West of which is also a small door; and to the South aisle by two plain arches. The floor is raised three steps above that of the nave; in the arch between them hangs a small brass Chandelier of three lights, and on the West end in the centre stands a small iron stove; the floor is of white pavement, and benches and chairs are placed on each side."

"The Nave is 40 feet 6 inches long by 19 feet 8 inches wide, and is covered with tiles. The pulpit stands on the North side near the East end and facing the West, and is painted to resemble wainscot. Below this the Nave is fitted up with oak seats having carved heads, on the top of which are small nozzas for candles; on the South side opposite the pulpit are a few pews; the seats are cleaned and oiled or varnished so as to look uniform and very neat. At the West end is a small gallery with an organ. On the front of this gallery are the arms of George the Third carved and painted all white; there are also a few pews under the gallery. The Nave is separated from the aisles by three plain arches on each side, which are supported by two pillars. The South aisle to the chancel is 24 feet 4 inches long, and 12 feet 2 inches wide; the ceiling flat on the North side. Here is the pew of the Acton Place family, filling up the whole of the two arches into the chancel; the floor is two steps above that of the aisle. At the East end and over the door into the Chapel hangs a hatchment. The rest of the aisle is 40 feet 1 inch long and 14 feet wide, covered with lead; it has pews on the South side. The South side of the porch has been fitted up as a vestry and at the outer door is placed a stove, and as far as the East window the floor is laid with deal, and on the East and West sides are benches, and at the North-East and North-West corners are cupboards, also a small day clock; the whole being very neat and convenient. Indeed the whole church is fitted up in the neatest manner, and is a pattern for all country churches. I have never met one in so complete a state of repair and comfort. The present Vicar, Mr. Bickersteth, has as I was informed been at a considerable part of the expense attending its present state."

The Church has a square embattled tower without a spire, and contains five bells which are thus inscribed:—

1. God save the King Miles Graye made me 1684.
2. Thomas Gardiner fecit 1747.
3. Miles Graye made me 1663.
4. Miles Graye made me 1679 Nicholas Kenington.
5. John Thornton made me 1716.

"The chief entrance at present into the Church is through the tower. So much has the comfort and convenience of the congregation been consulted, that in the North-West corner of the churchyard a place of accommodation has been erected for those who during divine service may have to satisfy the calls of nature."

"There are numerous monuments and historical inscriptions."

"In the Chapel or Dormitory, at the East end of the aisle and against the East wall, is a very large and costly monument of various kinds of marble, consisting of a kind of altar of white and black marble, on the top of which reclines the full-sized figure white-streaked marble, of a man in a Court dress, embroidered coat buttoned down to his knees, over which his stockings are rolled, his shoes square toed. He is lying on a mattress and pillow, resting on his right arm, looking upwards, and resting his left hand on his thigh. On his head is a full bottom wig, and around his neck a cravat, the ends of which hang down a considerable length. Behind his feet sits a female figure of full size, a cloth or veil covering her head and hanging down, her left hand up to her ear, the head leaning forward. Her right hand holds a handkerchief and rests on her knee. The figure is very heavy and the attitude awkward; for she appears as if scratching her ear, or stopping it with her hand to prevent her hearing something unpleasant to her. Against the wall, at the back of these figures, is a large table of black streaked marble in a frame surmounted by a composite pediment which is supported by four pilasters with Corinthian capitals. Over the pediment are three potbellied arms, very clumsy and ugly, and on the dark marble slab are the arms of the Jennens and Guidott families."

The following inscription (the letters of which have been cut by an inferior hand) appears on the marble base or front slab immediately beneath the figures:—

"To the Memory of

"Robert Jennens of Acton Place in the County of Suffolk Esquire fourth son of Humphrey Jennens of

MONUMENT IN ACTON CHURCH
TO THE MEMORY OF ROBERT JENNENS.

Warwickshire esq^r who dyed the 25th of February 172$\frac{3}{4}$ in the 54th year of his age leaving only one son William Jennens by Anne his Wife only daughter and heir of Carew Guidott of Hampshire esq^{re} He purchased the estate and began the house.

"This monument was erected by his Wife who also built this Chappel.

"She died the 24th December 1761 aged 85 and is deposited in the family vault under the Chancel adjoining to this Chapell with the remains of her said husband.

"The above-named William Jennens died on the 19th of June 1798, in the 98th year of his age is buried in the same Vault with his father and mother and his memory thus perpetuated by his particular direction."

Respecting this inscription the following is found in Vol. 2, East Angliæ :—

"Jennens family of Acton Suffolk.

"I am very desirous to obtain an exact Copy of the inscription on the monument erected to the memory of Robert Jennens in Acton Church Suffolk previous to April 1805. On that day the inscription consisted of 471 letters, and between that day and the 8th July the statuary cut 165 more letters making in the whole 636 letters. But when I copied every letter on the monument on the 11th April 1859 I found only 454 letters. In 1805 there was a splendid achievement of arms on the top of the monument, for painting and gilding which the artist was paid £2 - 16 - 0, but there was none in 1859.

"JAMES COLEMAN,
"22 High Street Bloomsbury."

The following is a Copy of the "Artist's" bill for painting and gilding the Acton Monument, and cutting additional letters thereon in 1805 :—

"The Right Honourable Lady Baroness Howe.
"Dr. to Richard Long, Ballington, Essex.
"1805.
"April 22.—To painting and guilding the coat of Arms on the Monument in Acton Chapple £2 16 0
To cutting and painting 165 Letters on the marble table at 2¼ p letter 1 14 4½
To painting the old inscription 471 letters at 1^d p letter 1 19 3
To coppying the inscription and Jorneys to self and man after the above work 1 0 0

£7 9 7½

"2^d Stamp.
"1805 July the 8th
"Received the contents of the Bill affixed as above.
£   s.   d.
7 ,, 9 ,, 7½
"RICH^D LONG."

Mr. Coleman's letter and Richd. Long's bill agree in detail.

The bill and receipt have been copied from a book which appears to have been a portion of "John Haywood's accounts," and can be produced if required. Since 1859 the number of letters must have been AGAIN altered, if Mr. Coleman's statement be correct.

If Mr. Coleman be accurate as to the difference of 82 letters in the inscription between the years 1805 and

1859, then for a certainty the present cannot be the original inscription. Then why has it been tampered with? The omission of 82 letters implies the concealment of a fraud, and indeed there are not wanting reasons to warrant the assumption.

The funeral of William Jennens is thus noticed in the *Ipswich Journal* of June 30th, 1798 :—

" Friday last the remains of Wm Jennens Esqr of Acton Place were interred in the family vault at Acton Church with much funeral pomp. The body was conveyed in a hearse decorated with escutcheons, and four mourning coaches, with several private carriages in which were neighbouring gentlemen, followed in the procession. The concourse of people assembled on the occasion was very great indeed. On opening the vault the coffins of his father and mother only were found therein, the former of whom had been buried 73 and the latter 37 years. We understand that no will has yet been discovered, but about £20,000 was found in money and bank notes at his town and country houses, and also a key to the chest containing his mother's plate and valuables, which is deposited at Child's the bankers, and has never been opened since her decease. No accurate idea can be formed of the amount of his property, as he never until very lately employed any regular steward. He was very regular and exact in all his accounts, insomuch that he even noticed his household bills exceeding their usual weekly amount. His expenses were supposed not to be above £3000 a year, although his property it is thought cannot fall short of

£2,000,000. *What relations survive him,* IF ANY, *is at present unknown,* but his immense wealth is expected to open a wide field for litigation."

"The amount of the property left by the late Wm. Jennens is stated to be as follows:—

In the Public Funds—

Bank Stock	£35,000 at 123	£45,000
5 per cents.	30,000 ,, 75	22,500
4 per cents.	24,000 ,, 60	14,400
3 per cents.	50,000 ,, 50	25,000
3 per cents. reduced ...	50,000 ,, 50	25,000
Long Annuities per annum	2,000 ,, 14	28,000
South Sea Stock	15,000 ,, 50	7,500
South Sea New Annuities	20,000 ,, 50	10,000
South Sea Old do.	20,000 ,, 50	10,000
East India Stock	23,890 ,, 150	35,835
	£269,890	£223,285

Cash—

Dividends due Bank	£100,000	
Cash do.	57,000	
Ditto at Batson's	19,000	
Ditto at Child's	6,000	
East India Dividends... ...	7,000	218,000
London Assurance—Interest on 400 shares...	3,000	
South Sea Anns.	26,000	
Landed Property per annum, 26,000 at 25 years, purchase		650,000
		£1,091,285

" The late Mr. Jennens outlived three generations of heirs, and the Honourable Mr. Curzon inherits a will made fifty years before he was born."

The *Gentlemen's Magazine* of June 19th, 1798, at pages 627 and 628, gives the following notice of the death of William Jennens:—

"In his 97th year, William Jennens, of Acton Place, near Long Melford, Suffolk, and of Grosvenor Square, Esq. He was baptized in September, 1701, and was the son of Robert Jennens, Esq., *aide-de-camp* to the Great Duke of Marlborough (by Anne his wife, daughter and heiress of Carew Guidott, Esq., lineally descended from Sir Anthony Guidott, Knight, a noble Florentine, employed on sundry embassies by King Edward the Sixth), and grandson of Humphrey Jennens,* of Erdington Hall, County of Warwick, Esq., lord of the Manor of Nether Whitacre, in that county, in 1680, and an eminent ironmaster at Birmingham. King William the Third was Godfather to the late Mr. Jennens, and amongst the valuables discovered in his house is a silver ewer, which was the present from that monarch at his baptism. He had been page to George I., and during the long period of his life remained a bachelor, more given to penuriousness than hospitality. Of course his accumulations magnified even beyond his computations. He was the last of the annuitants of the Exchequer Tontine of £100 a share,

---

*In fact nobody at the time really knew who he was, and this information was no doubt supplied by Lady Andover and Mr. Lygon. But it is now proved that he was not the grandson of Humphrey Jennens.

for which he had received £3,000 a year for many years past. He had property in almost every fund; and such was his immense wealth that the dividends on most of his stock have not been received since 1788, nor the interest on his mortgages for a long time. In his iron chest, the key of which could not be found till after a long search, hid in a mortgage deed were bank notes of the year 1788, to the amount of £19,000, and several thousands of new guineas. About £20,000 were found in money and bank notes at his town and country houses, and also a key to the chest containing his mother's plate and valuables, which is deposited at Child's the bankers, and has never been opened since her decease. He is reported to have always kept £50,000 in his banker's hands for any sudden emergency, and had not drawn a draft on the bank for the last fourteen years. He never till very lately employed a regular steward. Not many years since an eminent attorney, of Suffolk, who happened to be present, offered his assistance at his audit, thinking the fatigue too great for Mr. Jennings' age; but he was answered, 'What, do you think I can't write?' He was very regular and exact in all his accounts. It appears that he has had very faithful servants, who will be all well provided for. A will was found in his coat pocket, sealed, but not signed, which was owing, as his favourite servant says, to his master's leaving his spectacles at home when he went to his solicitor for the purpose of duly executing it, and which he afterwards forgot to do. By this testamentary instrument, in which

GOPSAL HALL.

John Bacon, Esq., of the First Fruits Office, was a residuary legatee, the whole of the property was intended to be totally alienated from the channels into which it has accidentally fallen. The most material sufferers by Mr. Jennens dying without a will are the Hanmer family, of Bettesfield Park, in Flintshire, and Holbrook Hall, in Suffolk. Mr. Jennens' own aunt was mother to William Hanmer, Esq., of the Fenns, first cousin of the late Sir Walden Hanmer, of Bettesfield, the Fenns; and his descendants (particularly those residing in Suffolk) have most certainly been in the greatest habits of friendship with Mr. Jennens. The above-mentioned William Hanmer, Esq., married his first cousin, Miss Jennens, of Gopsall, by whom he had a daughter, Hester, who married Asheton (now Lord Curzon), by whom he had a son, the Honourable Penn Asheton Curzon, M.P. for Leicestershire, who married Lady Sophia Charlotte Howe, daughter of Earl Howe, and died Sept. 1st, 1797, leaving an infant son, George Augustus William Curzon, who was born May 14th, 1788, and is now heir-at-law to all the real estate (which he had possessed for 73 years).* His personal property devolves on his cousins, William Lygon, Esq. (grandson of Mrs. Hester Hanmer, aunt of the deceased), and Mary, relict of William Howard, commonly called Viscount Andover (eldest son of Henry Bower Howard, late Earl of Suffolk and Berks.), grand-

---

* This information must have been supplied by the parties who then claimed the property. There were then no known relations who were in a position to oppose the claim.

daughter of Dame Anne Fisher, also aunt of the deceased.* Thus his most incalculable wealth merges into three individuals possessing previous fortunes almost immense. On the 29th his remains were interred in the family vault at Acton Church." (See *Gentleman's Magazine*, vol. 68, p. 627, 628.)

The following is from "Gillingwater's Collection," Acton :—

"The property of the late William Jennens, Esq., is said to exceed two millions sterling, and there is reason to apprehend he died intestate.

"An executed will was found among his papers at Acton, in which he had devised some comparatively inconsiderable legacies to gentlemen in the neighbourhood. Lord Curzon's family was expected to be the inheritors of his immense property, and his Lordship after visiting Acton, and giving orders for the funeral, set off for the house of the deceased in Grosvenor Square, London, to discover, if possible, a testamentary instrument. During the long period of his existence, he remained a bachelor, more given to penuriousness than hospitality. Of course his accumulations magnified even beyond his powers of computation. He is reported always to have kept £50,000 in his banker's hands for any sudden emergency, and never drew out the dividends of his funded property (the bulk of his fortune) till half a year after they were due. He served the office of Sheriff for his county in 1754."

---

* Inquiries are being made as to the alleged descent of William Lygon and Lady Andover from Humphrey Jennens.

GOPSAL CHAPEL.

Betham, in his " Baronetage of England," says of William Jennens, of Acton Place, in the County of Suffolk, "that he was the only son of Robert Jennens, who was the younger son of *John Jennens*, the great Warwickshire ironmaster. His mother, whose maiden name was Guidart, was maid of honour to Queen Mary, and he had the honour of a royal sponsor in the person of King William." This glimmering of the truth of William's descent from a Robert Jennens, who was the son of a *John Jennens*, is nearer the truth than any of Betham's contemporaries. He was in fact the son of Robert the younger, who was the son of Robert the elder, who was the son of *John Jennens No. 2*. We will now proceed with an account of the dismantling of Acton Place. In Davy's Suffolk collections fo. 22, we find the following advertisement :—

" To be sold by auction, on the premises of Mr. Thyne, on Tuesday, the 22nd March, 1825, and the two following days, in lots :—

" All the valuable building materials of the mansion house called Acton Place, near Sudbury, Suffolk, consisting of excellent brickwork, stone copings, steps, paving, chimney-pieces, about 400 feet of Portland paving with black dots, very superior marble chimney-pieces, about fifty squares of good yellow deal floor boards, fifteen squares of oak floor boards, sixty squares of clean bottom floor, 16,000 feet of wall framings and wainscots, numerous deal and wainscot-moulded doors with superior dressings, wainscot sashes, frames,

I

shutter and fittings, several tons of lead in flat sinks, pipes, flushings, &c., and numerous useful materials deserving the particular attention of gentlemen and builders."—*Ipswich Journal, March 5th,* 1825.

And in the same journal of the 30th April, 1825, appeared the following advertisement :—

" To be sold by auction, by Mr. Thyne, on the premises, 17th May, 1825, the second part of the valuable building materials of the mansion house called Acton Place, to be taken down and cleared away by the purchasers.

" Comprising excellent brickwork and tiling, stone copings, sill corners, Portland paving with black dots, rafters, girders, beams, quarters, floor joists, and many tons of lead in gutters, flats, sinks, pipes, flushings, &c. and numerous useful materials deserving the attention of gentlemen and builders."

From the quality and quantity of the materials sold one may infer the size and extent of the building.

If the parties who committed this act of Vandalism had any other motive than concealment, it must have been that of avarice. They were already immensely rich, and apparently discontented, they sought to add to their ill-gotten wealth the money to be realized by the sale of the materials.

About this time many people began to make enquiries respecting the next of kin, and even the identity of Lady Andover was called in question.

In the *Gentleman's Magazine*, p. 755, we find the following letter addressed to Mr. Urban, the editor or proprietor :—

"Lady Andover, one of the heirs of the late Mr. Jennens! Behold here, Mr. Urban, a new proof of the *accuracy* and attention of our modern peerage writers. In a peerage published in 1790, by Owen, &c., article, 'Earl of Aylesford,' the said Lady Andover is said to have died in 1767. 'Mr. Kearsley's complete Peerage,' published in May last, faithfully copies the same falsehood under the same article; but in the article, 'Earl of Suffolk,' he permits her ladyship to live ten years longer, and says she died 28th May, 1777. Is it the design of these publications to communicate information, Mr. Urban? or for what purpose are they printed?"

If, then, Lady Andover died in 1777, how could she have administered in 1798? This problem has to be solved. In the "Suffolk Peerage" (which may be inspected at the Parliament Office, House of Lords, for 5s.) she is stated to be living in 1780. Was this really the fact? We shall see.

In the same Magazine, vol. 73, part 1, page 287, is the following notice:—"March. At her house at Elford, county Stafford, in her 87th year, Mary, Dowager Viscountess Andover. She had lived *secluded* from all society but that of her relations and most intimate friends for the last 20 years, and has died immensely rich both in landed and personal property. The amount of the latter is unknown. Her landed property was the gift of her son, the Earl of Suffolk, for her life, and entailed on his sister the Hon. Mrs. Howard. Of her personal property a considerable part came to her as one of the heirs-at-law of the rich Mr. Jennens, of Acton Place. (Vol. lxviii., 627, 755). During the course of her long life she was universally respected, and disposed of more and without ostentation, of larger sums to those whose comfort she wished to promote, or whose wants required assistance, than perhaps were ever given before by any individual. She was sister to the late Earl of Aylesford, and married William, Lord Viscount Andover, son of Lord Suffolk, who died before his father. Her children by him were the Earl of Suffolk, formerly Secretary of State, and the Hon. Mrs. Howard, married to the Hon. Richard Bagot, now Mr. Howard, brother to the late Lord Bagot. Lord Suffolk, in 1777, married his first cousin, Lady Charlotte Finch, eldest sister to the Earl of Aylesford. The Hon. Mrs. Howard has but one daughter to inherit the vast property of her grandmother, Lady Andover. A considerable legacy is supposed to be left to the present Earl of Aylesford."

Further remarks will be made on the subject of her will.

We will now resume the pedigree of Humphrey Jennens and his children, from two of whom the present owners trace their descent.

John Jennens (No. 1) married 1st, his cousin Mary Jennens, the eldest child by whom was John (No. 2); he married 2ndly, Joyce Weaman, the eldest son by whom was Humphrey.

The children of the first marriage had portions given to them by their father in his lifetime, but the bulk of the property owned by John (No. 1) at the time of his death was given by his Will to the children of the second marriage.

Humphrey married Mary Millward, by whom he had 6 sons and 6 daughters, viz.:—Ann, Justine, Henry, Charles, Mary, Esther, John, Humphrey, Elizabeth, Robert, Phelicia, William.

Ann, the eldest of these children, is said to have been the grandmother of Lady Mary Andover.

Esther, the sixth child, is said to have been the grandmother of William Lygon.

So Lady Mary Andover and William Lygon claimed to be entitled to administer as next of kin.

Charles, the fourth child, is said to have been the great-great-grandfather of Earl Howe, who, as heir-at-law, claimed the real estate.

And Robert, the tenth child, was said to have been the Father of William Jennens, of Acton Place, the intestate.

The Will of Humphrey Jennens is dated the 14th February, 1689, and was proved on the 18th July, 1690. He describes himself as "Humfrey Jennens, of Erdington, in the County of Warwick, Esq." There is a legacy to his Wife, Mary Jennens, and also a devise for her jointure and in recompense of her dower and thirds. After the death of his wife he devises certain landed estates unto Sir Charles Holt, Sir Clement Fisher and Sir John Bridgman, Baronets, and Robert

Burdett, Esq., their executors, administrators and assigns, for and during the term of 500 years, upon trust, to raise by sale or mortgage or out of the rents of the said lands, the legacy payable to the widow and also the sum of £2000; and to pay unto his sons John Jennens, Humphrey Jennens, Robert Jennens and William Jennens, £500 a piece, to be paid to them within the space of 12 months after Testator's death. Remainder to the issue of any son in the event of death. But if his son Charles, or any other of Testator's sons to whom the remainder and inheritance of the said lands were limited or devised, should pay or cause to be paid the said sums or legacies intended to be raised by the trustees, that then the said term of 500 years shall cease. Testator then devises the reversion expectant on the said term of 500 years unto his eldest son Charles Jennens and his heirs male. In default to his son John Jennens and his heirs male, and in default to his son Humfrey Jennens and his heirs male, and in default to his fourth son Robert Jennens and his heirs male, and in default to his son William Jennens and his heirs male, and in default of lawful issue to Testator's own right heirs for ever. These are the only sons mentioned in the Will.

There are certain other devises to Testator's said sons. Then there is a legacy to Humfrey Jennens of £1500, with remainder to John, Robert and William. Then a devise to Robert of land purchased by Testator of his brother Edward. Also a legacy to Robert of £2200, with remainder to John, Humfrey and William.

Then follows a devise to William Jennens, with remainder to John, Humfrey and Robert; and a legacy to William of £2500, with remainder to John, Humfrey and Robert. Legacy to his daughter, Mary Jennens, of £4000. Legacy to Hester of £4000, and to Pheletia £4000, but subject to forfeiture or reduction by reason of marriage without the consent of the mother.

[We must here again refer to Elizabeth, one of the daughters of Humphrey Jennens, who by becoming a Roman Catholic and marrying without consent became an outcast, not even being mentioned in the Will.]

In the event of forfeiture or reduction, such sums to increase the portions of those daughters who married with their mother's consent; remainder to the sons— John, Humfrey, Robert and William.

Each of Testator's said daughters to have £100 a year for her maintenance, in addition to her portion, until such portion became payable.

After making certain provisions for securing the payment of legacies, there is the following Proviso :—

"Provided furthermore and my will and mind further is that my Executor by and with the consent and approbation of the said Mary my Wife shall or may upon request of my son Robert Jennens (who is already placed *an apprentice*) pay any sum or sums of money to my said son Robert not exceeding the sum of one thousand pounds to *adventure and employ in trading during his apprenticeship* although he shall not be then of the age of one and twenty years and that his receipt of the same shall be a sufficient discharge to my executor notwithstanding his nonage."

[This Robert is at one and the same time represented to be an apprentice in trade, to be a military student, and to be of the Middle Temple. He is said to have been *aide-de-camp* to the Duke of Marlborough, and to have married Anne Guidott and to have been the father of William of Acton.]

Testator empowers his executor to make advances to the younger sons. Then there is a specific bequest to his widow. Gift of Erdington Hall to his widow, with remainder to his son John, and in default of issue to Humfrey, and in default of issue to Robert, and in default of issue to William, and in default of issue to Testator's heirs. Gift for life to widow of household goods at Erdington Hall; remainder in succession to John, Humfrey, Robert and William, and Testator's heirs. Gift to Charles for the repairs and furniture of the house, and for stocking the estate at Erdington. Further pecuniary and specific bequests to his widow. Legacy to his daughter, Lady Fisher, of £20; to Sir Clement Fisher, £20; to his granddaughter, Mary Fisher, £50; to Mrs. Esther Booth, £10; to his cousin, Dorothy Parkes, forty shillings. Then follow legacies to his servants, and to his brother Edward, £10. Testator then directs certain lands to be purchased and the profits to be given to certain poor people in Birmingham. His executor is directed to pay to Testator's brother Abraham the sum of four shillings a

Erdington Hall, Country Residence of John Jennens, of Birmingham, 1653.

week for life. He leaves all his ironworks, and stock and effects belonging to same, to his son John, who shall abate £1000 of his legacy. Devise of estate at Over Whitacre to Robert, reduced to an annuity of £20 payable by John, who is to have the ironworks there. Testator devises unto his said said son   Jennens, his executors, administrators and assigns, the manor of Forshaw ats Foshaw, in the parish of Solyhull, in the County of Warwick. Empowers his executors and overseers to raise £1500, by sale of timber, towards the payment of legacies, and for that purpose bequeaths unto them Sansome Woods. Other payments and disbursements to be paid out of Testator's personal estate. Bequest of residue to the younger sons—John, Humphrey, Robert and William,—in equal shares with remainders in succession. Bequest of books to Charles. Testator's widow to be guardian, and in the event of her death, Charles to be guardian. Charles to be sole Executor. Sir Charles Holt, Sir Clement Fisher and Sir John Bridgman, Baronets, and Robert Burdett, Esq., to be overseers of Testator's Will.

Throughout this will the word "Humphrey" is spelt "Humfrey," and this was one of the main objections to the claim of the descendants of Elizabeth Jennens, who married Jeremiah Smith. It seems to have been the mode of spelling adopted both by John (No. 1) and his son Humphrey; but Humphrey's son Humphrey, in his Will dated 14th Octr., 1714, spells Humphrey with a "ph."

As for the usual mode of spelling names, see Office Copy Will of Ambrose Jennens,* the brother of John Jennens (No. 1). After spelling his own name "Jennens," he proceeds *inter alia* "Item I doe give and bequeath unto my cozen and Godsonne Ambrose *Jennins* Sonn of my said brother Ambrose *Jennyns* the sum of thirtie pounds." Spelling, then, is no criterion as to the identity of a persons handwriting. Why, even the grandson of King James the II., commonly known as The Young Pretender, was equally as careless in his spelling, writing his grandfather's name as "Gams," and for "humour," "umer." Numerous similar instances among men of rank and even learning could be given, but it is submitted it will be unnecessary.

But Ambrose Jennens, further on in his Will, writes for Jennens "Jennynes," as follows:—"Item I doe give and bequeathe unto my lovinge Brother John *Jennynes* the sume of twentie pounds." Four various ways in one will!

We now notice the children of Humphrey Jennens in their order of birth.

Ann married Sir Clement Fisher, and had issue Mary, who married The Right Honourable Earl of Aylesford, and had issue Mary, who married William Howard Viscount Andover. According to various peerages this lady is represented to have died at three different dates, namely:—1767, 1777, and 1803. This

---

*Ambrose Jennens, although a dealer in ironware, is described in his will as a Cordwainer.

lady is a mystery. In the Suffolk peerage she is represented to be living in 1780. Again, it is said that she died in 1803, and her Will to have been proved by her daughter, The Hon. Frances Howard, the wife of Richard Howard, Esq. (formerly Bagot).

As regards Lady Andover's Will, it may be observed that if education be a criterion to the position of any one (as was argued in the case " Hood *v.* Beauchamp") then that rule ought in all fairness to be applied to this Will. The Will of Mary Howard, commonly called Viscountess Andover, is dated the *twentith* day of March, 1795, three years before the death of William Jennens, of Acton Place. The best plan will be to give the copy of the Will and Codicil *verbatim et literatim* :—

" This is the last Will and Testament of me Mary Howard commonly called Viscountess Andover. I leave my daughter The Honble *Francess* Howard sole executrix and residuary legatee of all my personal estate after the payment of all my debts and funeral expenses and such legacies as I shall mention in this my will or any codicil annexed to it and it is also my Will and desire that any Box Letter or Parcel directed by me as a Remembrance to any friend may be *dilivered* to them. I do most earnestly Will and desire that all moneys justly due from me to my eldest daughter the Honble Catherine Howard as may be seen by her accounts kept by me may be so secured and made the most of for her that with the friendship and *advise* of her sister Mrs. Howard and her good brother in law Mr. Howard she may never want any of the comforts and *necessarys* of life that she is capable of enjoying. I will and bequeath to my said daughter Catherine Howard my Gold Watch made by Thompson it was her Father's Watch and I hope she will receive it as a kind remembrance from us both I will and bequeath to my daughter Frances Howard all *portrate* pictures and plate belonging to me at the time of my death the latter (viz) the plate nevertheless subject to my debts and the discharge of this my will in case I do not leave money sufficient to pay them I leave to my dear daughter Charlotte Countess Dowager of Suffolk my Gold Repeating Watch made by Graham with all the seals and lockets annex'd to it I leave to all my servants that live me me at Elford at the time of my death a years wages over and above what may be owing to them at the time of my death and I leave Eight hundred pounds to be *equaly* divided between my four old servants Wm Giles, Frances Mandy, Sophia Weston, and John Edwards in case they live with me at the time of my death, I leave to the poor of the parish of Elford Five hundred pounds to be disposed of to or for them by my Executrix in whatever manner she may judge may be most *advantagious* for them I desire to be buried in the *Vaul* with my husband Lord Andover in the Church Yard at Elford and in the most decent and private manner possible attended only by my good *Tennants* and servants and I will to have a Leaden Coffin. This is my last Will and Testament revoking every former Will or Wills I have ever made and to which I set my hand and seal this *twentith* day of March 1795.

"MARY ANDOVER. (L.S.)

"Witnesses Clemintina Maria Elizabetha Sawsey, John Sneyd.

"On Mr Wm *Jenins* death a great *personal comes* to me he *died* the 19th June 1798 and *least* I should die before I could make another *more enlarged* Will I leave a Codicil annexed to this by me

"MARY ANDOVER."

What does the reader think of the above short Will and Codicil containing nearly a score instances of misspelling and inaccuracies? Would he not imagine a Judge to say (as in the case "Hood *v.* Beauchamp") that it was plain to him that the Will and Codicil were not in the handwriting or the production of Viscountess Andover: that nothing could be more unlikely than to suppose that a lady, the wife of a peer of the realm, educated in the manner in which ladies of her position must have been educated, should have made so many mistakes.

But the Will and Codicil are not the only subjects of suspicion.

In 1788 "Complete Peerage" states she died in 1767.
,, 1794 " Kearsley's   ,,   ,,   ,,   1767.
,, 1796 " Ditto   ,,   ,,   ,,   1767.
,, 1809 " Ditto   ,,   ,,   ,,   1767.
,, 1790 " Owen's   ,,   ,,   ,,   1767.
,, 1790 " Kearsley's. ,,   ,,   ,,   1777.
Last of all it is published as in - - 1803.

Why all this mystery? Is it possible that the Peerage writers were all incorrect before 1803? If so, why were not the mistakes rectified? In justice to the children and friends this certainly should have received prompt attention, for in the absence of contradiction, it is venial to believe that her Ladyship died either in 1767 or 1777, and to suppose that some person of inferior station and education was imposing on her family.

One of the reasons frequently given for believing that persons have predeceased their friends, is the omission of the persons' names in their friends' Wills.

In " Hood v. Beauchamp " the mere fact of the omission of Elizabeth's name in the Wills of her father and her brothers and sisters, was deemed conclusive proof of her death in the life-time of her father.

Apply the like test to Lady Andover. Her father's Will is dated 1767, her brothers Will 1777, her sister Ann's Will 1793, her sister Elizabeth's Will 1793; there are also many other Wills of her relations, but in none of these Wills is she ever mentioned. What is the inference?

Who was the mysterious lady who administered to the estate of William Jennens the intestate who died in 1798?

A copy of the Will, together with the Affidavit of Mr. Richd. Howard, Memorandum of Probate and Administration, *de bonis non* will be found in the appendix.

The next child of Humphrey's is Justine, who it is said died in infancy.

The like is said of the next child Henry.

The next child is Charles, and as it is from him that Earl Howe says he is descended, that will be the subject of inquiry.

Charles Jennens married Elizabeth Burdett and had issue seven children, one of whom was named Elizabeth who married William Hanmer, Esq., and had issue Esther who married Asheton Curzon, and had issue Penn Asheton who married Baroness Howe, who had or is said to have had issue Richard William P. Curzon, Earl Howe.

The Claimants dispute in toto the right of Humphrey's descendants to any portion of the property real or personal left by William Jennens of Acton, he and the Claimants being descended from John (No. 2) the Brother of Humphrey: so that Humphrey's line is too remotely related to have a legal claim. True they possess by a pseudo legal right, and if proceedings be commenced there is little doubt but that they will plead the Statute of Limitations. It certainly would not be a righteous act to plead the Statute if they see the validity of the claim, and they ought to remember that they as hereditary legislators are responsible for good government, and that good government is inseparable from justice. Let it then be hoped that they will on seeing that there is a good and *bonâ fide* claim, admit it, and be prepared to behave as honest men.

The next child is Mary, who it seems never married. Her Will is dated the 29th September, 1707, and was proved on the 4th January, 1708.

It is as follows :—

"In the name of God amen. I Mary Jennens being in perfect health sound memory and judgment (praised be God therefore.) Doe make and ordain this my last Will and Testament in writing in manner and forme following (that is to say.) I give and bequeath to my

brother Charles Jennens fifty pounds. To my brother
John Jennens fifty pound. To my brother Humfrey
Jennens fifty pound. To my brother *Robert* Jennens
fifty pound. To my brother William Jennens fifty
pound. To my sister Hanmer fifty pound. To my
cosin Frances Gower senior 1 hundred pounds. To
my neece Mary Jennens of Gopsall my diamond ear-
rings To my Godaughter Betty Jennens 4 hundred
pounds To Cresswell Wilks if in my service 1 hundred
pound and all my cloaths. To the poor in Aston
Parish I leave fifty pound I give to my cosin Gowers
6 daughters 10 pound a peece. All the rest of my personall estate I give and bequeath to my sister Felicia
Jennens whom I make constitute and ordain my sole
executrix of this my last Will and Testament. In
witness whereof I have hereunto set my hand and seale
in the 7th year of the raigne of our Soveraigne Lady
Queen Ann 1707 the 29th day of September Sealed
signed and published in the presence of Richard Cope
—Cresswell Wilks."

On the 4th January, 1708, Robert Jennens and
Anne his wife attend and identify the handwriting of
Mary Jennens, the Testatrix. Again it must be asked,—
was the language then used by Robert Jennens, the
language of a brother identifying his sister's handwriting, or that of a distant relative? (We say the
latter).

The next child is Esther who married William
Hanmer, and had issue Susannah who married Reginald Pindar Lygon, and had issue William Lygon (1st

K

Earl of Beauchamp) who married Catherine Denn, and had issue William Lygon (2nd Earl Beauchamp) and John Reginald Pindar Lygon (3rd Earl Beauchamp).

The next child is John, whose Will is dated the 5th October, 1726. In his Will he is described as of the City of Bath, in the County of Somerset, Esq. He mentions his wife Elizabeth Jennens; Sir Clement Fisher, baronet; his brother William Jennens; his sisters Hanmer, Phelicia; his brother Charles and his daughters Ann and Mary; he also mentions his nephew William Jennens, the son of his late brother *Robert*.

The next child is Humphrey, whose Will is dated the 14th October, 1714. In it he mentions his brothers Charles, John, Robert and William, and his sisters Hester, Phelecia. Testator appears to have been the first member of the family who spelt his name "Humphrey" with a "ph."

The next child is Elizabeth, who it is said married Jeremiah Smith. Her descendants were unsuccessful in their attempt to establish their claim in 1836. The principal points against them were the name of "Humphrey" written in a book and spelt with a "ph" instead of an "f," and the supposed neglected education of Elizabeth, who it was surmised was not Elizabeth the daughter of Humphrey, for had she been, she would have received the education of a lady.

And now we come to Robert, upon the identity of whom hinges the whole case. In the first place there is no record of his birth, baptism, or marriage or burial, unless the marriage and burial of the other Robert are adopted as his. That he was the son of Humphrey, and was married, and had a son William, is clearly shewn by his father's, his brothers' and his sisters' Wills. Was this Robert the person who proved the handwriting of Mary Jennens previously mentioned? Was he the Robert of Erdington mentioned in the conveyance of the Acton Estate?

It is admitted by all parties interested, that the late William Jennens, of Acton Place, was the son of Robert and Anne his wife, who was the daughter of Carew Guidott, and the only critical part of the case is as to the parentage of the said Robert Jennens. Was he the grandson of John (No. 2), or the son of Humphrey the half-brother of John (No. 2).

The present owners of the property maintain that Robert, the father of William of Acton, was the fourth son of Humphrey Jennens, who was the eldest son of John (No. 1) by his second marriage with Joyce Weaman.

The Claimants on the other hand contend that the said Robert was the son of Robert (who married Jane Truelock), and who was the son of John (No. 2), who was the eldest child of John (No. 1) by his first marriage with his cousin Mary Jennens.

It is strange that whilst the Claimants have so many records in proof of the descent of the said Robert Jennens, the present owners have only the doubtful inscription on the monument to establish his identity. No one can produce a certificate of his birth or baptism, notwithstanding large rewards have been offered, and indeed no record as to the identity of this Robert being the son of Humphrey has ever been found. That he was apprenticed in trade it is clear from his father's Will; but that he would at the same time be a military cadet and qualifying for the position it is said he subsequently held is scarcely credible; and at this time also he is described as of the Middle Temple.

Humphrey Jennens was born in 1627, and died in 1690; he was therefore 63 years of age at the time of his death.

In 1700, it is said that Humphrey's son Robert was married to Anne Guidott; but the application for that marriage licence states that the age of that Robert was then 28 years.

If, then, Humphrey's son Robert and the Robert mentioned in the application for the marriage licence be identical, it follows that Robert at the time of Humphrey's death would be only 18 years of age, and would then probably still be an apprentice in trade. How, then, about his becoming *aide-de-camp* to the Duke of Marlborough? If on the expiration of his apprenticeship in 1693 he left his trade to study the science of war, he would scarcely have the time to accomplish that object.

Queen Anne reigned from 1701 to 1714, during which time the Duke of Marlborough obtained his brilliant victories at Blenheim, Ramillies, Ondenarde, and Malplaquet. Could this Robert have served during Marlborough's campaign? It is not proved that he had any military training, or that he became a soldier.

Let it be granted that Robert's circumstances being suddenly changed by the death of his father, in 1690, and that he did not serve the last three years of his apprenticeship in trade—granted also that by reason of his altered circumstances he for a time resided with his brother Humphrey in the Middle Temple, and that he afterwards became a military officer—it will only prove a remarkable coincidence of two kinsmen of the same name being similarly circumstanced.

If such be the case, it will account for one of the traditions of the family as to the disappearance of this Robert Jennens. Soon after having acquired his fortune, he espoused the cause of Prince James or the Chevalier, and went to France, where he not only assisted the Prince with funds, but undertook to serve him in his attempt to regain the throne. By dint of perseverance he qualified for a commission, and was present at the battle of Sheriff Muir, in November, 1715. At the end of the short and unsuccessful campaign he fled, and being a proscribed rebel, he was concealed and maintained by his friends until his death.

All the incidents of this Robert's life are vague, shadowy and traditional.

How different are the incidents of the life of Robert the grandson of John (No. 2)! We will now follow them.

Robert Jennens, the grandson of John (No. 2), 1672, June 18th. He was baptized at Sutton Courtney in Berkshire.

1700, Oct. 16th. Special licence obtained for the marriage of Robert Jennens (who is described as of the Middle Temple, and as 28 years of age). The marriage licence is expressed to be for a marriage at St. Giles'-in-the-Fields.

1700, Oct. 17th. Marriage of Robert Jennens, of the Middle Temple, to Anne Guidott, daughter of Carew Guidott. This register is found among several registers at Westminster Abbey.

1705. Robert Jennens and Anne (his wife) are plaintiffs in a foreclosure suit in respect of property under Carew Guidott's will. By this will Charles Jennens and William Guidott are appointed trustees.

1708. Bargain and sale of Acton Place to Humphrey Jennens and Anthony Guidott (Robert Jennens, of Bedford Row, being the real purchaser.—See William Jennens' will.) A Robert Jennens of Erdington Hall (supposed to be the son of Humphrey Jennens the half-brother of John (No. 2) is a party thereto. No wife is mentioned. At this time Robert Jennens the father of William the intestate was, with his wife, living at his country seat, Ham Common, Kingston-on-Thames. This can be proved by office copies of proceedings in Chancery, to which Robert and his wife were parties.

1708 Robert Jennens and Anne (his wife) jointly prove the handwriting of Mary Jennens in terms which it is scarcely possible would be used by a brother as regarded his sister. In this will, Mary leaves £50 to her brother Robert. No notice is taken of her brother's wife, although Anne, if she were her sister-in-law, must have been well known to her, and worthy, one would think, of some token of affection. Robert Jennens, who with Anne (his wife) proved the handwriting of Mary Jennens, was, as has been seen, her cousin once removed.*

1710. Robert Jennens was buying and selling property at Sutton Courtney.

1719. Robert Jennens is described in various documents as of St. Andrew's, Holborn.

1726. Robert Jennens died, leaving his wife Anne and his only child William him surviving, and was buried at Acton, near Long Melford, on the 5th March, 1726. About this time another Robert Jennens died, and was buried at *St. Andrew's, Holborn*, on the 25th March, 1726.

In March 1726, administration of his effects were granted to his son William Jennens, and therein Robert was described as of *St. Andrew's, Holborn.* Mystery upon mystery! Was Robert Jennens of Bedford Row, who died of apoplexy in 1726, and who, it is said, is buried at Acton, the same Robert Jennens who, it is said, is buried at St. Andrew's, Holborn—or

---

* Brothers
John—Humphrey
|
Robert cousin Robert
|
Robert "once removed."

is the latter entry in the register of St. Andrew's, Holborn, a record of his death only?

But it little signifies to the Claimants where Robert Jennens the grandson of John (No. 2) is buried; they have, it is submitted, deduced their descent from John (No. 2), and they are prepared with the necessary documents in proof of the same.

If these documents are authentic (and undoubtedly they are), they prove their descent from John Jennens who died and was buried at Birmingham in 1653. As follows:—William Jennens the intestate, was the son of Robert Jennens the younger (variously described as of St. Andrew's, Holborn and of Bedford Row) and Anne his wife, and that Robert Jennens the younger was the son of Robert Jennens the elder and Jane his wife, and that Robert Jennens the elder was the son of John (No. 2) and Jane his wife, and that John (No. 2) and his half-brother Humphrey (the father of the *other* Robert) were the sons of John (No. 1) who died in 1653.

Can anything be clearer than this pedigree?

William Jennens then of Acton, having died a bachelor and intestate, and without parents, or brothers, or sisters him surviving, his nearest male representative would not only be entitled to Letters of Administration, but would also be his heir. William's father was an only surviving child, therefore his eldest great-uncle (John No. 3) and his descendants are the first entitled. Failing them, the next great-uncle is William; but he died without issue. With William the intestate,

Robert the elder's line is extinct, and there now only remain the descendants of Roger, the next great-uncle, to prove that the property of William of Acton has been withheld from them by fraud, or that they are still entitled to it by virtue of an existing trust.

Of Phelicia and William, the remaining children of Humphrey Jennens, it is only necessary to say that it is believed they died without issue.

It is a notable fact that long before the discovery of the family Bible, it had been considered necessary to obtain certain certificates of baptisms, marriages, and burials. When the Bible was found, with a number of old documents in a wooden chest, these certificates and the entries in the Bible were compared and found to agree. That the Bible is an heir-loom is beyond doubt, but it is unfortunate that an earlier discovery of it was not made.

Can it be suggested that the Bible has been surreptitiously obtained, or that the entries therein are forgeries? If they be forgeries, would not the writer have been careful to avoid such a mistake as "boy" instead of "by?" And after the repeated instances of erratic spelling exhibited by the office copies of the Wills, is it possible that any objection can be taken on this account? If then the Bible entries can be relied upon as evidence, and the Claimants fairly deduce their descent in the manner intimated, they, and they only, as the descendants of John (No. 2), the great-grandfather of William Jennens of Acton, are, it is submitted, entitled to the property.

THE END.

APPENDIX.

EXTRACTED from the Principal Registry of Her Majesty's Court of Probate.

" (In the Prerogative Court of Canterbury.)"

" IN THE NAME OF GOD AMEN the five and twentieth day of February in the yeere of our Lord God one thousand six hundred fiftie and one I JOHN JENNENS of Birmingham in the County of Warwicke Ironmonger being in good and perfecte health and memorie (praised be God the Lord for the same) yett considering the frailetie of man and to thend my temporall estate and blessings where with the Almightie hath blessed me shalbe divided among my Children kynsfoulke and friends Doe make and ordaine this my last Will and Testament in writeing hereby annullinge and revoking all former Wills and Testaments whatsoever And first I commend my Soule into the hands of Almightie God my Creator Saviour and preserveher and my bodie to be buried in the pish Church of Birmingham aforesaid Trusteing and beleeveing that through the mercye of Almightie God and the alone meritts of my Saviour the joyes of his eternall Kingdome Imprimis I give and devise all that messuadge or tente wherein I now dwell or inhabite in Birmingham

aforesaid and the barnes buildings gardens backesides
lands tenements and hereditaments whatsoever there
onto belonginge and all that Croft or close in or neare
onto the New Streete in Birmingham aforesaid purchased of Mr William Warde with the barnes and out-
buildings thereupon and allsoe all that little pcell of land
at the lower end of my garden which I lately purchased
of Robert Baylies and allsoe all that Crofte or close of
pasture comonly called Maddocke crofte in or neare the
New Streete aforesaid and allsoe all that close or pasture comonly called Colehouse wth the barne standeing
thereoupon and allsoe all those three closes or pcells of
land comonly called Hungarhills which said Colehouse
and Hungarhilles are lyeing and being in Edgbaston in
the said Countie of Warwicke onto my loveing Sonne
Humfrey Jennens and the heires of his body lawfully to
be begotten and for wante of such issue Then I give
and devise the said Colehouse and Hungarhills To my
loveing Sonne Joseph Jennens and the heirs of his
bodie lawfully to be begotten and for want of such
issue to my Sonne Edward Jennens and the heires of
his bodie lawfully to be begotten and for wante of such
issue to the heirs of my bodie on the bodie of my late
deare and tender Wiefe Joyce Jennens lawfully to be
begotten and for wante of such issue To the right heires
of me the said John Jennens for ever And for want of
heires of the Bodye of the said Humfrey Jennens I
give the said messuadge and lands in Birmingham
aforesaid onto my said Sonne Edward Jennens and the
heires of his bodie lawfully to be begotten and for want

of such issue to my said Sonne Joseph Jennens and the heires of hys bodie lawfully to be begotten and for want of such issue to the heires of my bodie and the bodye of my said Wiefe Joyce Jennens lawfully begotten and for want of such issue To my right heyres for ewer Item I give and devise all these my severall leases estates interests and termes of yeares yetto come of or in a Certayne Meadow comonlie called Barnes Meadow lyeing and being in Duddeston in the said Countie of Warwicke and in certayne barnes croftes closes and landes in Birmingham aforesaid wch I hould of Roberte Phillippes and allsoe in certayne parcells of Meadowe grounde in Piddinge Meadowe in Codington in the said County of Warwicke which I hould of Mr. Ambrose Phillippes and also a certaine house and in Birmingham aforesaid which I hould of the Governors of the Free Scoole of Birmingham aforesaid onto my said Sonne Humfrey Jennens his executors administrators and assigns payeing the respective rents and performing the respective covenants in my respective leases concerning the same And my Will and meaning is And I doe hereby will and devise that if my daughter Sara Jennens shall lyve onto her full age ofone and twentie yeeres Then I doe give and devise onto my said daughter Sara Jennens the some of five hundred pounds to be then payd onto her And if the said Sara shall marry before she accomplish that age by and with the consente and good likeinge of my executor and overseers of this my last Will and Testament here after named or of the greater number of them Then

the said five hundred pounds shalbe payd to her within
five months after her marriage and if shee shall marry
before that age without the consent of my said
Executor and overseers orof the greater number of
them then the said five hundred pounds shall not be
paid to her and then I give only twentye pounds provided always nevertheless and upon express condition
that if the said Sara Jennens shall depart this life before
her sayd legacie or legacies some or somes of money
hereinbefore willed given or devised to her shalbe
due as aforesaid that then her said legacye or legacies
so devised or given to her as aforesaid shalbe
remayne and be paide equally Pte and Pte like to such
of my said Children Humfrey Jennens Joseph Jennens
and Edward Jennens as shall be lyeveing at the decease
of the said Sara Item I doe give and devise onto my
said three Sonnes Humfrey Joseph and Edward Jennens
my servall estates leases interests and tearmes of yeares
yetto come ofor in the Forges Water courses and
highway and Aston Furnace with all Edifices barnes
yards wayes passages watercourses pooles dames
libertyes comodities wastes closes lands tenements
meadowes and appurtenances vnto the said forges and
last mentioned premises belongeing or in anywise apper-
taining or to or with the same or any parte thereof lett
sett used or enjoyed as pte and pcell thereof all which
said forges Aston Furnace and last mentioned premises
are scituate lyeing and being in Hivles in the County
of Staff[d] and in Curdington and Aston in the said
County of Warwicke are now in the tenure or occupa-

ASTON HALL.

tion of mee the said John Jennens or of my assignes or undertenants or some of us and allsoe one hundred loades of Charcole and thirtie Tunes of rough Pigge Iron (my said Sonnes their executors and assigns payeing after my decease the servall yearly rents reserved for the same and performing of the covenants during the continuance of the said leases menconed Item my Will and mynd is and I doe hereby declare that my said Sonne Edward Jennens his Executors and assignes shall have hould and enioye all my lease estate time and terme of yeares yetto come and unexpired which I have or oughte to enioye of or in one Messuage or tenemente and certayne lands tenements Meadowes pastures and hereditaments with the appurtenances scituate lyeing and being in Wedgeburge West Bromwich and Walsall some or any of them in the said County of Stafford nowe or late in the tenure or occupation of one John Carter his assignes or vndertenants or some of them Item though I have formerlye Well and sufficiently preferred and advanced my Son Abraham Jennens according to my estate notwithstanding that hee hath been very vndutiful to vnto mee yett for the better lyvelyhood of him and hys I doe hereby Will and devise that if my said Sonne Abraham shall within two months next after my decease by a good and sufficient deed in lawe in writing under his hand and seal vnto my Execator of this my Will Will and Testament all All manner of accovns suites causes of accoons claymes and demannds whatsoever and shall not at any time hereafter clayme or demand any pte of my estate or any

L

righte title or interist in or vnto the same or any pte thereof that my said Executor by the advice of my overseers of this my last Will and Testament or of the greater pte of them within the space of one yeare next after my decease shall bestowe in purchase in some lands tenements or hereditaments the sume of three hundred and fiftie pounds of lawful money of England and my Will is that the said lands tenements and hereditaments shalbe at the chardge of my said Executor settled and estated vpon some pson or psons and his and their houses in trust and for the benefit of my said Sonne Abraham for hys lief and after hys decease then upon or of the first Sonne of the body of the said Abraham lawfully begotten or to be begotten and of the heirs of the body of the first sonne lawfully to be begotten and for want of such yssue of the second sonne of the bodie of the said Abraham lawfully begotten and to be begotten and of the heires of the bodie of such second sonne lawfully to be begotten and for wante of such issue, of the third Sonne of the bodie of said Abraham lawfully begotten or to be begotten and of the heires of the bodie of such third Sonne lawfully to be begotten and for wante of such issue of the fowerth fifth sixth and seaventh sonnes of the bodie of the said Abraham lawfully to be begotten one after another as they shall be in prioritie of age and senioritie of Birth and not jointly and of the heires of their sevral bodyes lawfully to be begotten. And for want of such issue of the first second third and all other the daughters of the Bodie of the said Abraham lawfully begotten and to be begotten and of the heires of such daughters lawfully to be begotten And for wante of such issue of the heires of my bodie on the bodie of my deare and tender Wiefe Joyce Jennens lawfully begotten and for want of such issue of my right heires for ever And my Will is that my said Executor shall allsoe disburse the some of fiftie pounds of lawfull money in buyeing Cattle and other necessaries for flocking of the said lands tenements and hereditaments when they shalbe soe bought as aforesaid which stocke my Will is shall be setled for the benefitt of my said Sonne Abraham by the advice of my said overseers or of the greater number of them And my Will is that vntill such time as the said fower hundred pounds shalbe layde outas aforesaid that my Executor shall pay after the rate of twentie pounds apeece tomy said Sonne Abraham for the presente mayntenance of him and hys Children Provided nevertheless and upon this expresse condition that if the said Sonne Abraham shall not make such release as aforesaid to my said Executor or shall clayme any pte of my or any other intereste right or title inor unto the same or any pte thereof that then my Will is that my said Executor shall not disbursse the said somes of three hundred and fiftie pounds and fiftie pounds or any pte thereof as aforesaid but that the same shall cease be voyde and of none effect and then and in such case I doe give to my said Sonne Abraham the only some of twentie pounds to be payde within a yeere after my decease Item I will and appointe that my said Executor by and with the consent of my said overseers or the greater pte of them out of and by such pte of my goods cattle Chattles household stuffe plate ready money stock wares in trade and debts owing or to be owing vntome as I shall hereinafter declare mencon or appoint within the space of three yeares after my decease buy lands or tenements of the yeerely value of   shillings of lawful money of England and that the same lands and tenements shalbe settled vnto and vpon my said Executor and overseers and some twelve of thenhabitants of Birmingham aforesaid such asmy said Executor and overseers or the greater pte of them shall thinke fitt and on and vntothe heirs of the said twelve inhabitants and Executor for ever and that the five last survivors of them shallon the like number being inhabitants there and their heires and soe continually when there shall be but five surviving feoffers theyshall make a new feoffment to others   To the use of them and others and their heires of like number   And in the said feoffments and assurances this pte of mysaid last Will and Testament tobe recited and that the yearly rent or value of the said last mentioned lands and Tenements shalbe imployed as hereafter in the psents is menconed or expressed   That is to say for the buying and making of gownes and Coates for the poore and aged people dwelling in Birmingham aforesaid and the towneborne tobefirst pferred before others the same to be bought and provided against Christide yeerely for ever and my Will is that noe poore pson shall have either gowne Or Coate two yeares togeather   And the poore people to goe to Church togeather on Easter day

Whidsonday and soe every other Sabbath day yeerely at the least for ever in their gownes and Coats and such of them as shall willfully neclecte haveing noe reasonable excuse to have noe more or other gownes or Coates And my Will is that vntill the said lands and tenements fiftie shillings shall bought fortie shillings yeerely yeerely shalbe takenout of the same pte as aforesaid for the buying and makeing of gownes and Coates And shall likewise buy within the same three yeares other lands and Tenements of the yeerely value of twentie shillings of lawful English money the same to bee stated on such a number of feoffeesents such manner from time to time for ever as the said lands and tenements of the fiftie shillings yeerely are herein appointed to be estated and the said yeerely value or rente of the said lands or tenements laste mentioned tobee yeerely given for ever on the one and twentieth day of December to the poore of Birmingham aforesaid being Townes borne And my Will and meaning is that vntill the said lands and tenements laste menconed shall be boughte twentie shillings yeerely shalbe taken out of the aforesaid pte to be yeerely given vnto the said poore Item I give vnto my loveing Mother in lawe Dorothy Item three pounds to buy hera a gownde Item I give vnto my my Daughter in lawe Jane Jenens five pounds to buy her a gownde and to John Jenens sonne of my late Sonne John Jennens five pounds to be payd vnto hym at hys age of one and twentie yeeres Item I give vnto my grande Childe Jane Jennens when shee shalbe of the age of eighteen

yeares tenn pounds and to my grand childe William
Jennens when hee shalbe of the age of One and twentie
yeeres tenn pounds Item I give vnto Ales the nowe
Wiefe of my Sonne Abraham Jennens five pounds and
to John Jenens sonne of the said Abraham when hee
shalbe of the age of One and twentie yeeres twentie
pounds and to Joyce daughter of the said Abraham
Jennens when shee shall accomplish the age of eighteen
yeeres Tenne pounds and to Ales Daughter of the said
Abraham Jennens when shee shalbe of the age of
eighteen yeeres five pounds Item I give vnto ewy of
my godchildren two shillings five pence apeece Item
I give vnto my servante Thomas Miller Thirteene
pounds five shillings eight pence and tomy servante
William Jennens tenn pounds Item I give vnto the
said Thomas Myller five pounds a yeere dureing such
time as hee shalbe imployed in the like way as hee now
is over above hys wages or Sallary which shalbe allowde
hym by my said Sonne Humfrey Item I give vnto all
my servants that shall dwell with mee at my decease
Ten shillings apeece and to all my servants that shall
goe with my teames ewy of them five shillings apeece
Item my Will and meaning is and I doe will and
appointe that if any losse shall happen in any of my
goods or chattels that then the same shalbe borne
equally and indifferently by ewy of my said legatees
wch are or weare to have the same or any pte or pts
thereof And my Will and meaning is and I doe further
will and appointe that if any question strife or debate
shall arise or happen for aboute or concerneing my

devise or bequest or other matter or thing in this my
last Will and Testamente menconed or contcigned that
the same shalbe heard ended and determined by my
said overseers or the greater number of them and I doe
straightly charge my Executor and children and every
of them willinglie and readdilie to abide and perform
such Will and determination soe to be made as aforesaid Item my Will and meaning is and I doe hereby
desire will and appointe that all my goods Cattell
Chattels plate readie money stocke and wares in trade
and debts owing vnto mee my debts owing by mee and
my legacies guiftes funeral chardges and expences being
first payde and deducted shalbe parted and divided into
fower equall parts by my said Executor and overseers
or the greater number of them as equally and indifferently as they or the greater number of them can or may
to their best abilitie the moietie or an half thereof I doe
give and devise vnto my said Sonne Humfrey Jennens
and the other moietie or half thereof I doe hereby alsoe
give and devise vnto my said Sonns Joseph Jennens
and Edward Jennens and to my said daughter Sara
Jennens chargeing them to bee ruled ordered and directed
by my said overseers or the greater number of them
toucheing or concerneing any question doubte or matter
toucheing or concerneing any legacy or thing in this my
laste Will and Testamente spied or conteyned and
yeerely And I doe hereby make constitute and ordaine
my said sonne Humfrey Jennens sole Executor of this
my last Will and Testamente And I doe nominate and
appointe my loveing son in lawe William Booth Esquire

my Kinsman Thomas Peeke and Thomas Ailsbury Abraham Allen and Richard Banner Overseers of this my last Will and Testamente in writing their best care and paynes to see this my last Will and testament duely and fully pformed And I doe give toervy one of them for their paynes to bee taken therein fortie shillings apeece Item my Will and meaning is and I doe hereby will and appointe that the severall and respective legacies and legacies hereby given Willed and appointed to my said Children Joseph Jennens Edward Jennens and Sara Jennens evry or any of them shalbe imployde or vsed to and for his her and their beste proffitt and increase that can or may be made or raysed for or by the same soe longe as the same or any of them or any pte or pts of them or of any of them shalbe unpayde or not satisfied vnto him her them or any of them In witness whereof I the said John Jennens thelder have to this my laste Will and Testament conteyned in Tenne sheetes of paper all written with one hands sett my hand and seale the day and yeare firsts above written

"THIS Will was proved at Westm the tenth day of March in the yeare (according to the English accomp^t one thousand six hundred fiftie three before ye Judges for Probate of Wills and granting Admons lawfullie authorized By ye Oath of Humfrey Jennens Sonne of ye said deceased and sole Executor named in the said Will to whom was committed Adstracon of the goods chattels and Credits of the said deceased hee being sworn by virtue of a commission truely to Administer the same."

EXTRACTED from the Principal Registry of Her Majesty's Court of Probate.
" (In the Prerogative Court of Canterbury.) "
" IN THE NAME OF GOD AMEN the fourteenth day of February in the second year of the Reign of our Sovereign Lord and Lady William and Mary by the Grace of God King and Queen of England Scotland France and Ireland Defenders of the Faith &c Anno gz Dem One thousand six hundred and eighty nine I Humfrey Jennens of Erdington in the County of Warwick Esquire being of perfect and disposing memory and understanding praised be God for the same do make and declare this my last Will and Testament in manner and form following that is to say First I commend my Soul to God that gave it hoping by the only merits of my only Saviour Jesus Christ to be made partaker of Everlasting Life in his Heavenly Kingdom and my body to the earth from whence it came to be decently interred at the discretion of my Executor hereinafter named And as for my worldly Estate I dispose thereof as followeth that is to say Imprimis I give and bequeath unto my dear and loving Wife Mary Jennens the sum of Two hundred and fifty pounds of lawful money of England and the sum of One hundred pounds more of like money which I have borrowed or received of my Wifes money both the said sums to be paid by my Executor out of my personal Estate within twelve months next after my decease Item I give and devise unto the said Mary my Wife for and during her natural life all that my Manor or

Lordship of Nether Whittacer in the County of Warwick with the rights member and appurtenances thereof And all and every my Messuages Cottages Lands Tenements tythes and hereditaments with the appurtenances situate lying and being in the Parishes Liberties territories or precints of Nether Whittacre Holloughton Drakenedge Kingsbury Coton and Maxstock and in every or any of them in the County of Warwick aforesaid for her jointure and in full recompense and satistion of her dower and thirds and also in exchange lew and instead and for a full recompence and satisfaction for all and every the messuages cottages lands tenements and hereditaments in Cudworth Dunton Wishaw Wiggin Hill Sutton otherwise Sutton Coldfield otherwise Kings Sutton Minworth Waterorton als Wateroverton and Merivale and in every or any of them in the County of Warwick aforesaid which were formerly settled by me upon the said Mary my Wife for her jointure at my Marriage with her according to the liberty and power to me limited or reserved by my Marriage Settlements and from and after the decease of the said Mary my Wife then I give and devise all the said Manor or Lordship of Nether Whittacre and all and every my said messuages cottages lands tenements tythes and hereditaments in Nether Whittacre Holloughton Drakenedge Kingsbury Coton and Maxstock and every or any of them unto my trusty and well beloved friends S$^{r.}$ Charles Holt S$^{r.}$ Clement Fisher and S$^{r.}$ John Bridgeman Baronets and Robert Burdet Esq$^{re.}$ their executors admors and assigns for and during the term and unto the full end and term of five hundred years from thenceforth next ensuing and following fully to be compleate and ended without impeachment of or for any manner of waste upon trust and confidence and to the intent and purpose that they or the survivors or survivor of them or the executors or admors of such survivor by and out of the rents issues and profits of the said Manor Lands and premises or by sale or mortgage of the said Manor Lands and premises or any part thereof or of any Wood timber or trees thereupon growing or by such other ways and means as they in their discretion shall think most proper and convenient shall levy and raise the sum of Two thousand pounds of lawful money of England and shall pay and dispose thereof in manner following that is to say unto my Sons John Jennens Humfrey Jennens Robert Jennens and William Jennens five hundred pounds a piece to be paid unto them respectively within the space of twelve months next after my Wifes decease And my Will and mind is that if one or more of my said younger Sons shall depart this natural life without issue before the end of the said twelve months That then and in such case the respective sum or sums of five hundred pounds before ordered appointed or intended for him or them so dying without issue shall be paid unto the survivors or survivor of them But if any of them shall depart this natural life and leave issue behind them which shall be living at the end of the said twelve months after my Wife's decease Then my Will is that the issue of him or them so dying

respectively shall have the same and not the survivors
or survivor of my said sons. Provided always nevertheless and my will and mind further is that if my Son
Charles Jennens or any other of my Sonnes to whom
the remainder and Inheritance of the said manor lands
and premises is herein limited or devised do and shall
well and truly pay or cause to be paid all and every
sum and sums of money before mentioned or intended
to be raised by the said trustees unto such person and
persons and at such time and times and in such manner
and form as the same are before mentioned or directed
to be paid by the said trustees as aforesaid   That then
the said term of five hundred years shall cease end
determine be void and of none effect anything in this
my Will contained to the contrary thereof in any wise
notwithstanding and for and concerning the remainder
reversion and inheritance of all and every the said
manor messuages cottages lands and premises expectant
upon the said term of five hundred years I give and
devise the same unto my eldest Son Charles Jennens
and the heirs males of his body lawfully begotten or to
be begotten and for default of such issue then to my
Son John Jennens and the heirs male of his body lawfully to be begotten and for default of such issue then to
my third Son Humfrey Jennens and the heirs males of
his body lawfully to be begotten and for default of such
issue then to my fourth Son Robert Jennens and the
heirs males of his body lawfully to be begotten and for
default of such issue then to my fifth Son William
Jennens and the heirs males of his body lawfully to be

begotten and for default of such issue then to my right
heirs for ever in exchange lieu and stead and in full
recompense and satisfaction for the said messuages
cottages lands tenements and hereditaments in Curdworth Dunton Wishaw Wigging Hill Sutton otherwise
Sutton Coldfield otherwise King's Sutton Minworth
Waterorton otherwise Wateroverton and Merivale
aforesaid and also of certain other lands and tenements
in Duddeston and Over Whittacre which were formerly
settled by me upon the issue male of my body upon the
body of the said Mary my Wife by my marriage Settlements but are now otherwise disposed of by this my
Will according to and in pursuance of a power to me
limitted or reserved by my said marriage Settlements
Provided always nevertheless and my Will and mind is
that if my said Son Charles Jennens or the heirs males
of his body or any other of my Sons in remainder or the
issue male of their bodies shall disturb or molest my
said Son John Jennens or the heirs of his body or any
other of my younger Sons or their issue to whom I shall
give or dispose of the said premises in Curdworth
Dunton Wishaw Wigging Hill Sutton Coldfield Minworth Waterorton Merivale Over Whittacre and
Duddeston or any of them or any part thereof in his or
their quiet enjoyment thereof respectively according to
the intent and meaning of this my Will or shall not
upon the reasonable request costs and charges of my
said Son — Jennens or the heirs of his body or any
other of my younger Sons or his or their issue to whom
I shall give and dispose of the same respectively by this

my Will do and execute any lawful and reasonable act or acts thing or things devise or devises conveyance or assurance in the Law for the full and firm settling conveying and assuring the same or any part or parts thereof unto such person or persons respectively And of or for such Estate and Estates and in such manner and form as I shall give devise or despose of the same by this my Will respectively that then and in such case the aforesaid gift and devise of the said Manor of Nether Whittacre and the said Messuages Cottages lands and premises in Nether Whittacre Holloughton Drakenedg Kingsbury Coton and Maxstock and every of them as to my said Son Charles Jennens and my other younger Sons in remainder respectively and the respective issue male of their bodys begotten and to be begotten as aforesaid shall cease and be absolutely void and of none effect And then and in such case I give and devise the said Manor or Lordship of Nether Whittacre and all my said Messuages Cottages Lands and premises in Nether Whittacre Holloughton Drakenedge Kingsbury Coton and Maxstock and every of them after the end or other determination of the said term of five hundred years in manner and form following (that is to say) in case my Son John Jennens or the heirs of his body or any other of my younger Sons in remainder or their issue to whom I shall by this my Will give devise or dispose of my Estate in Duddeston aforesaid shall be molested or disturbed in his or their quiet enjoyment thereof according to the intent and meaning of this my Will then and in such case I give and devise all those my severall messuages houses lands and tenements with their and every of their appurtenances situate and being in Nether Whittacre aforesaid in the several and respective tenures used or occupations of Widow Hasterly Widow Greenway William Cranes John Charles and William Warwick their respective assigns or undertenants unto my said Son John Jennens and the heirs of his body lawfully to be begotten and for default of such issue then I give and devise the same unto my Sons Humfrey Jennens Robert Jennens and William Jennens and the heirs of their several and respective bodies lawfully to be begotten to be equally divided amongst them for and instead of the said premises in Duddeston And in case my Son Humfrey Jennens or the heirs of his body or any other of my younger Sons in remainder after him or their issue to whom I have or shall by this my Will give devise or dispose of my Estate in Curdworth Dunton Sutton Coldfield Wishaw Minworth Coleshill and Waterorton and in every or any of them shall be molested or disturbed in his or their quiet enjoyment thereof or of any part thereof so as the same shall not or may not be quietly and peaceably enjoyed according to the true intent and meaning of this my Will then and in such case I give and devise unto my said Son Humfrey Jennens and the heirs of his body lawfully to be begotten All that my messuage farm or tenement and all and every the Lands and Tenements thereunto belonging or therewith usually occupied or enjoyed situate and being in Nether Whittacre aforesaid and formerly in the tenure or occupation of the Widow Mitchell her assigns or undertenants and now or late in the tenure or occupation of Edward Brabbins his assigns or undertenants And also all those my several messuages houses farms lands and tenements with their and every of their appurtenances situate and being in Nether Whittacre aforesaid now or late in the several and respective tenurss uses or occupations of Edward Langley Thomas Hollier Thomas Wright John Harrison and William Meatham their respective assigns or under tenants To have and to hold the same unto my said Son Humfrey Jennens and the heirs of his body lawfully to be begotten And for default of such issue then I give and devise the same unto my Sons John Jennins Robert Jennins and William Jennins and the heirs of their respective bodies lawfully to be begotten to be equally divided amongst them to take as tenants in common and not as joint tenants instead of the lands and Tenements in Curdworth Dunton Sutton Coldfield Wishaw Minworth Coleshill and Waterorton aforesaid which I have or shall have by this my Will devised unto and intended for them And in case my Son Robert Jennens or the heirs of his body or any other of my younger Sons in remainder after him or his or their issue shall be molested or disturbed by my eldest Son or the heirs of his body or any of my other Sons after him in remainder or his or their issue in the quiet and peaceable enjoyment of my Estate in the Parishes or Precincts of Merivale and Over Whittacre or either of them so as the same or any part thereof shall not be quietly or peaceably enjoyed according to the true intent of this my Will Then and in such case I give and devise all that my Capital Messuage or Manor house in Nether Whittacre aforesaid and all the barns stables Outhouses edifices building gardens orchards fold yards curtilages and appurtenances thereunto belonging or therewith used And all the several closes fields grounds and meadows called by the several names of the Tanners yard Rocketts field Quinton field Rayle field Brook Meadow Barnefield Pearetree field Stride spring Long field Well field Little Parke Meadow great Parke Meadow upper Parke Meadow Conduitt Wood Waltons Wood Brown's Wood and Spring Park with the appurtenances All which grounds lye near unto the said Manor house in Nether Whittacre aforesaid unto my said Son Robert Jennens and the heirs of his body lawfully to be begotten And for default of such issue Then I give and devise the same unto my Sons John Jennens Humfrey Jennens and William Jennens and the heirs of their several and respective bodies lawfully to be begotten to be equally divided amongst them to take as tenants in common and not as joint tenants for and instead of the Lands and tenements in Merivale and Over Whittacre aforesaid which I intended for my said Son Robert Jennens Item I give and devise unto my said Son John Jennens and the heirs of his body lawfully to be begotten all and every my Messuages cottages lands tenements and hereditaments with the appurtenances in the Parishes Lordships or Precints of Birmingham and Duddeston and in either of them in the

M

County of Warwick and in Halesowen in the County
of Salop   And for default of such issue of the body of
any said Son John Jennens to be begotten   Then I
give and devise the same unto my Sons Humfrey
Jennens Robert Jennens and William Jennens and the
heirs of their several bodies lawfully to be begotten to
be equally divided amongst them to take as tenants in
common and not as joint tenants   And for default of
such issue   Then I give and devise the same unto my
right heirs for ever nevertheless my Will and mind is
that if my Son Charles Jennens shall depart this
natural life without issue male of his body begotten
whereby my said Son John or his issue shall come to
inherit my Estate limitted unto or settled upon my Son
Charles after my decease that then and in such case
the gift and devise aforesaid of my said messuages and
Lands in Birmingham Duddeston and Halesowen unto
my said Son John and the heirs of his body as aforesaid
shall cease and be void and that then the same shall be
enjoyed by and I give and devise the same unto my
said other younger Sons Humfrey Robert and William
and the heirs of their several and respective bodies to
be equally divided amongst them as aforesaid   Item I
give and bequeath unto my said Son John Jennens the
sum of Three thousand pounds of lawful money of
England to be paid unto him by my Executor out of
my personal Estate within the space of twelve months
next after my decease   Item I give and devise unto my
Son Humfrey Jennens and the heirs of his body lawfully
to be begotten all and every my messuages cottages

lands tenements and hereditaments with the appurtenances in Curdworth Dunton Sutton Coldfield Wishaw Meriworth Coleshill and Waterorton and in every or any of them And for default of such issue of the body of my said Son Humfrey Jennens Then I give and devise the same unto my said Sons John Jennens Robert Jennens and William Jennens and the heirs of their several and respective bodies lawfully to be begotten to be equally divided amongst them to take as tenants in common and not as joint tenants And for default of such issue Then I give and devise the same unto my right heirs for ever Item I give and devise unto my said Son Humfrey Jennens the sum of Two thousand and five hundred pounds of lawful money of England to be paid unto him by my Executor out of my personal Estate at his age of two and twenty years but if my Son Humfrey Jennens shall depart this natural life without issue before his said age of two and twenty years Then my Will and mind is that the said sum of Two thousand and five hundred pounds shall be paid unto and in such case I give and bequeath the same unto and amongst my three other younger Sons John Robert any William and the survivors and survivor of them equally share and share alike to be paid unto them respectively at their respective ages of one and twenty years each Son to have his respective share or part thereof at his and their respective age of one and twenty years and not to tarry or expect for the same until the other Son or Sons shall attain to the said age Item I give and devise all those my Meadows or Mowing grounds closes leasowes or pastures with the appurtenances commonly called or known by the names of the Sweetmoore or Sweetmoores and Little Huntnams lying and being in the Parishes or Precincts of Merivale or Coleshill in the said County of Warwick and all and every my Messuages Cottages Mills Lands tenements and hereditaments with the appurtenances situate lying and being in the Parishes libertys or Precincts of Over Whittacre and Shustocke and either of them in the County of Warwick aforesaid and all and every the messuages lands tenements and hereditaments with the appurtenances which I lately purchased of my brother Edward Jennens situate lying and being in or near unto the County of the City of Coventry and now or late in the tenure or occupation of the Widow Austen her assigns or undertenants unto my Son Robert Jennens and the heirs of his body lawfully to be begotten And for default of such isse then I give and devise the same unto my Son John Jennens Humfrey Jennens and William Jennens and the heirs of their several bodies lawfully to be begotten to be equally divided between them to take as tenants in common and not as joint tenants Item I give and bequeath unto my said Son Robert Jennens the sum of Two thousand and two hundred pounds of lawful money of England to be paid unto him by my Executor out of my personal Estate at his age of two and twenty years but if my said Son Robert shall depart this natural life without issue before his said age of two and twenty years then my will and mind is that the said sum of Two thousand and two hundred pounds shall be paid and in such case I give and bequeath, the same unto and amongst my other three younger Sons John Humfrey and William equally share and share alike to be paid unto them at their respective ages of one and twenty years each of them to have his respective share or part thereof as they shall respectively attain the said age And if any of them die before the said age without issue the survivors or survivor to have the whole Item I give and devise all and every my Messuages Cottages lands tenements and hereditaments with the appurtenances whereof I am seized of any Estate of Inheritance in Edgbaston Erdington and Washwood and in every or any of them in the county of Warwick aforesaid unto my Son William Jennens and the heirs of his body lawfully to be begotten and for default of such issue then I give and devise the same unto my three younger Sons John Humfrey and Robert and the heirs of their several and respective bodies lawfully to be begotten to be equally divided amongst them to take as tenants in common and not as joint tenants and for default of such issue then I give and devise the same unto my right heirs for ever Item I give and bequeath unto my said Son William Jennens the sum of Two thousand and five hundred pounds of lawful money of England to be paid unto him out of my personal Estate at his age of two and twenty years But if my said Son William Jennens shall depart this natural life without issue before his said age then my Will and mind is that the said sum of Two thousand and five hundred pounds shall be paid unto and in such case I give and bequeath the same unto and amongst my three other younger Sons John Humfrey and Robert and the survivors and survivor of them equally share and share alike to be paid unto them at their respective ages of one and twenty years each Son to have his respective share thereof as they shall respectively attain to the said age And furthermore I do by this my Will revoke and make void all and every the use and uses Estate and Estates limited or declared in and by my marriage Settlements as to for and concerning all my Estate in Curdworth Dunton Wishaw Wiggin hill Sutton Coldfield Miriworth Waterorton Merivale and Duddeston and every of them and do hereby declare that the feofees or grantees in the said Marriage Settlements named and their heirs shall from and immediately after my decease stand and be seized thereof unto and for the use and behoof of such of my younger Sons to whom I have by this my Will given and devised the same respectively and of and for such Estate and Estates and in such manner and form as I have given devised or disposed of the same respectively Item I give and bequeath unto my loving Daughter Mary Jennens the sum of Four thousand pounds of lawful money of England for her portion to be paid unto her within the space of twelve months next after my decease Item I give and bequeath unto my loving Daughter Hester Jennens the sum of Four thousand pounds of like money for her portion and unto my daughter Phelitia Jennens the like sum of four thousand pounds of like money for her portion and all and every

of the said respective sums to be paid unto such of my
Daughters as shall be above one and twenty years at
my decease within the space of twelve months after my
decease and to such of them as shall be under the said
age of one and twenty years at my decease to be paid
unto them respectively at their respective ages of one
and twenty years or Marriage which shall next happen
Nevertheless my Will and mind is that if any of my
said Daughters shall marry without the consent and
approbation of their Mother in case she shall be then
living or of S$^{r \cdot}$ Clement Fisher and of my Son Charles
or the survivor of them if my Wife shall be then dead
then my will and mind is that such Daughter or Daughters soe marrying without such consent shall forfeit loose
abate or refund the sum of One thousand pounds out of
her or their respective portions and that the sum or
sums so forfeit lost abated or refunded shall be paid
unto such of my other Daughters as shall marry with
such consent for their incouragement and to increase
their fortune And my Will and mind further is that
if any of my Daughters shall have received her or their
portion and shall afterwards marry without such consent as aforesaid That then she or they so marrying
without consent shall immediately refund and pay back
again the sum of one thousand pounds a piece to be
paid unto such Daughter or Daughter as shall marry
with consent as aforesaid And my will and mind
further is that if any one or more of my said Daughters
shall depart this natural life unmarried before her or
their respective ages of One and twenty years that then

and in such case all and every of the sum and sums of money respectively intended for the portion or portions of her or them so dying shall be paid and I do in such devise the same unto my younger Sons John Humfrey Robert and William and the survivors and survivor of them which shall live to attain unto the age of one and twenty years equally share and share alike each Son to have and receive his share or part thereof as they shall attain the said age respectively Nevertheless my Will and mind is that the respective debts and legacies and funeral charges of her or them so dying shall be paid and discharged out of the portion or portions intended for them respectively so as the said debts Legacies and funeral expences doe not exceed the sum of One hundred pounds a piece And my Will and mind further is that each and every of my said Daughters shall have the respective yearly sum of One hundred pounds a piece of lawful money of England paid unto each and every of them respectively by my Executor out of my Estate for their respective maintenance and education and to augment their portions yearly and every year from my decease until their respective portions shall become payable and be paid as aforesaid the same to be paid within twenty days after Lady day and Michaelmas by even and equal portions the first payment thereof to commence and begin at such of the said days as shall next happen after my decease And I do hereby further declare that the aforesaid sums for maintenance and portions for my Daughters shall be and are in full recompence and satisfaction of and for all and every sum and sums of money limited ordered or intended to be raised for their maintenance and portions by virtue of any former Settlement trust declaration or otherwise whatsoever Provided always and my Will and mind further is that if my said Son Charles Jennens or any other of my Sons after him shall depart this natural life without issue male whereby my said Son John Jennens or any other of my younger Sons shall become his heir or shall inherit the Estate which I have settled upon or shall descend unto my said Son Charles after my decease That then and in such case all and every the sum and sums of money which I have herein given or bequeathed unto such younger Son which shall come to inherit the Estate which I have settled upon my Son Charles shall be paid unto and distributed amongst such other of my younger Sons which shall live to attain to the age of one and twenty years equally share and share alike for the augmentation and increase of their portions Provided furthermore and my Will and mind further is that my Executor by and with the consent and approbation of the said Mary my Wife shall or may upon request of my Son Robert Jennens (who is already placed an apprentice pay any sum or sums of money to my said Son Robert not exceeding the sum of One thousand pounds to adventure and employ in trading during his apprenticeship although he shall not be then of the age of one and twenty years and that his receipt of the same shall be a sufficient discharge to my Executor notwithstanding his nonage and that my Executor shall or may raise and pay any sum or sums of money for placing apprentice or other preferment of any other of my younger Sons not exceeding the sum of Six hundred pounds a piece and that his or their respective receipt thereof shall be a sufficient discharge to my Executor for the same if my Executor and Overseers or the greater number of them shall think it proper and convenient to raise and employ any such sum or sums of money for any of my younger Sons as aforesaid And my will and mind is and I do hereby declare that such sum or sums of money as shall be paid or disbursed unto or for my said Son Robert or any other of my younger Sons respectively as aforesaid shall be reckoned and accounted as part of his or their respective portions and shall be deducted abated and allowed out of the same accordingly Item I give and bequeath unto the said Mary my dear and loving Wife one large silver bason and six silver plates which were bought with money given or left by her Father the same to be disposed of as she shall please And whereas I am possessed of and interested in a certain Messuage or tenement called Erdington Hall and the lands thereto belonging for a certain term of years determinable upon my decease and for one and twenty years afterwards as it now stands I do hereby give and bequeath all the said Messuage and Lands unto And my Will and mind is That the same shall be enjoyed by Mary my dear and loving Wife for and during so many years of the said term of One and twenty years as shall incur after my decease during my Wifes life if she so long long continue

and remain a Widow and unmarried after my decease
she paying the rents and performing the covenants
which are or ought to be paid and performed to Sir
Charles Holt the Owner of the said Estate and his
heirs And from and after my Wifes decease or remarriage which shall next happen Then I give and
bequeath the said last mentioned messuage and Lands
unto and my Will and mind is that the same shall be
enjoyed by my Son John Jennens and the heirs of his
body lawfully to be begotten And for default of such
issue then by my Son Humfrey Jennens and the heirs
of his body lawfully to be begotten And for default of
such issue then by my son Robert Jennens and the
heirs of his body lawfully to be begotton And for
default of such issue then by my son William Jennens
and the heirs of his body lawfully to be begotten And
for default of such issue then by the heirs of my body
begotten for and during all and every the rest and
residue of the said term of One and twenty years under
the rents covenants and agreements to be paid and performed unto the said Sir Charles Holt and his heirs and
as for and concerning all and every my household goods
being in my now Dwelling house in Erdington aforesaid
my Will and mind is that the same shall be enjoyed by
and I do hereby give and bequeath the use and occupation thereof unto the said Mary my Wife for and during
the term of her natural life if she continue so long unmarried after my decease she giving security to my Son
John or to such other person or persons as shall be
next in remainder and entituled to them by her own

bond within the space of three months after my decease
to leave the same unto such Sons as I shall hereafter
give and bequeath the same at the time of her decease
or remarriage with so little damage as may be by the
usage and employing thereof And from and immediately after the decease or remarrage of the said Mary
my Wife the which shall next happen Then my Will
and mind is that my said household goods shall be enjoyed by And I give the use and occupation only
thereof unto my Son John Jennens and the heirs of his
body lawfully to be begotten And for default of such
issue then unto my Son Humfrey Jennens and the heirs
of his body to be begotten And for default of such
issue then unto my Son Robert Jennens and the heirs
of his body lawfully to be begotten And for default of
such issue then unto my Son William Jennens and the
heirs of his body to be begotten and for default of such
issue To the heirs of my body for ever And in case
I shall depart this natural life before such time as I
have or shall have laid out and disbursed the sum of
One thousand pounds towards the repairing and
furnishing the house and stocking the Estate which I
have settled upon my Son Charles in such case I give
and bequeath unto my said Son Charles Jennens so
much money as will make up what I have or shall have
so disbursed to amount unto One thousand pounds
Item I give and bequeath unto the said Mary my Wife
my Coaches Coach horses harness and appurtenances
to her own use for ever and One hundred and fifty
pounds more than I have hereinbefore given or be-

queathed unto her Item I give and bequeath unto my loving Daughter the Lady Fisher Twenty pounds and to Sr Clement Fisher twenty pounds and to my Granddaughter Mary Fisher Fifty pounds to buy her a piece of plate and to my Sister Mrs Esther Booth ten pounds and to my Couzen Dorothy Parkes fourty shillings to buy her a ring in remembrance of me And unto my Servants Humfrey Raughton thirty pounds and to John Hopkins twenty pounds To William Jennens William Spencer Bartholomew Banner and Ralph Atkinson twenty pounds a piece and to Jeremiah Bordall my Servant twenty pounds and to Henry Titterton my Servant ten pounds and to Richard Cope ten pounds And to every other of my household Menservants five pounds a piece and to Elizabeth Raughton my Servant fifty pounds and to every other of my maid Servants which shall be living with me at my decease four pounds a piece and to every of my day Labourers which shall be employed by me at my decease twenty shillings a piece Item I give and bequeath unto my Clerks John Hadley Senr ten pounds and to Mr. Whitehall Matthew Linley Joseph Astley Charles Brunt and Samuel Wild my Clerks Twenty pounds a piece and to Samuel Wright my apprentice ten pounds and to my brother Mr Edward Jennens ten pounds All the said last-mentioned legacies to be paid so soon as may be after my decease nevertheless my Will and mind is that such of my said Clerks or Servants as shall be dead or not employed by me or removed from me or shall have given notice or warning of their departure

out of my service shall have no legacy nor benefit by
this my Will and prevent and avoid the trouble and
disturbance of distribution of money or dole unto the
poor at my funeral my Will and mind is that my
Executor within the space of one month next after my
funeral shall bestow and dispose of the sum of One
hundred pounds of lawful money of England unto and
upon the poor of the Parishes of Birmingham Birmingham Aston and other neighbouring Parishes and such
other places and in such manner and form as my said
Executor shall in his discretion think most proper and
convenient And Whereas my late father John Jennins
deceased did by his last Will and Testament in writing
give and bequeath the several sums of fifty pounds and
twenty pounds to be bestowed in Land the profits of
which said fifty pounds was to be distributed and disposed of for the buying of gowns and coats for poor
people in Birmingham yearly for ever and the interest
and profits of the said twenty pounds was to be disposed
of for some other charitable uses or to this or the like
effect And Whereas the said sums are not yet disposed
of according to the said Will my Will and mind is that
my Executor so soon as conveniently may be shall lay
out and bestow the sum of seventy pounds upon the
purchase of lands and shall settle order and dispose of
the rents and profits thereof according to the intent and
directions of my Father's Will and shall in the mean
time employ and dispose of the interest and benefit of
the said seventy pounds to the uses aforesaid And
furthermore I do hereby give and bequeath unto my

trusty and well beloved friends Sir Charles Holt Sir
Clement Fisher and Sir John Bridgeman Baronetts
and unto Robert Burdet Esqr the sum of Two hundred
pounds of lawful money of England to be paid at the
end of two years next after my decease in trust that
they and the survivors and survivor of them or the heirs
executors or administrators of such survivor so soon as
conveniently may be after the receipt of the said money
shall lay out and disburse the same upon the purchase
of an Estate in Land and shall settle the same Land
so and in such manner as that the rents issues and
profits thereof shall be for ever bestowed employed and
disposed of unto for and upon such Charitable uses
intents and purposes in the Parish of Birmingham in
the County of Warwick as by the said Sr Charles Holt
Sir Clement Fisher Sir John Bridgeman and Robert
Burdett or the survivors or survivor of them or the heirs
of such survivor together with the heir of my family
for the time being and his heirs or the greater number
of them shall in their prudence and discretion be
thought most charitable necessary and convenient for
the said Parish from time to time for ever nevertheless
my Will and mind is that the said sum shall not be
paid by my Executor unto my said trustees or any of
them until such purchase but shall be kept in my
Executors hands or set out at interest by him upon
good security until such purchase can be had and that
the interest increase and benefit thereof shall be disposed and employed to the same charitable uses   Item
my Will and mind further is that my Executor shall

weekly and every week from and after my decease upon request pay or cause to be paid unto my Brother Mr Abraham Jennens four shillings per week and every week during his natural life towards his maintenance and that my Executor shall and may detain and keep in his hands soe much money as may probably defray and discharge the said weekly payments any thing in this my Will contained to the contrary thereof notwithstanding And whereas I am possessed of and interested in several forges furnaces and Ironworks with the appurtenances which I conceive may be very proper and beneficial for my Son John Jennens having bred him up and employed him that way my mind and will is that all the said Ironworks and the stock of coles iron stone wood for coles and other things belonging to or used by with the said Ironworks shall be granted assigned transferred and turned over by my Executor unto my said Son John so soon as the same can conveniently be valued and apprized and that at a moderate and reasonable rate and price And my Will and mind is that he shall have the sum of One thousand pounds abated or allowed of the reall worth or value thereof he giving security to my Executor such as he and my Overseers or the greater number of them shall approve of for the residue of the money or value thereof over and above the said sum of One thousand pounds upon the turning over of the same and for the use or interest thereof at five per cent until the same shall be paid But if my said Son John shall refuse or cannot give such security upon the turning over of the said Ironworks as aforesaid Then my Will and mind is that the said Ironworks stock and premises shall be sold or otherwise disposed of to the best advantage so and in such manner as my Executor and Overseers or the greater number of them shall think most proper and most for the advantage of my Children And Whereas I have before by this my Will given and devised all my Estate in Over Whittacre unto my said Son Robert and the heirs of his body with remainder over to my other younger Sons and the heirs of their bodies whereof Pulbag Furnace or Ironwork is parte my Will and mind nevertheless is that my said Son John his heirs Executors or admors shall have and enjoy the said furnace or Ironworks called Pulbag Furnace with the appurtenances so long as he or they shall manage and employ my Ironworke and shall think it convenient for them to hold the said Pulbag furnace paying twenty pounds per annum to my said Son Robert and the heirs of his body and to such of my other younger Sons as are in remainder after him at Lady and Michaelmas by equal portions yearly and every year so long as my said Son John his heirs executors or admors shall hold or make use of the said furnace or Ironwork and allowing so much water for the use of Pulbag Mills as can convenintly be spared in such manner as now is and hath been formerly used and keeping and leaving the said furnace or Ironwork in repair any thing hereinbefore contained to the contrary thereof in any wise notwithstanding And my Will and mind is and I do hereby order and appoint that my said Son Robert shall at any

time after his age of one and twenty years upon request
and at the costs and charges of my said Son John make
and seal a Lease to him upon the said terms of the said
furnace or Ironwork for so long time as he shall please
to take the same   Item I give and devise unto my said
Son — Jennens his executors admors and assigns all
that the Manor or Lordship of Forshaw als Foshaw in
the Parish of Solyhull in the County of Warwick with
the rights members and appurtenances thereof and all
and every the Messuages houses cottages Barns Edifices
Buildings Meadows Pastures Feedings Waters Woods
Underwoods coppices coppice Woods libertys privileges
waste grounds lands tenements and hereditaments with
the appurtenances in the Parish of Solyhull aforesaid
which I hold by lease from Mr Robert Gibbons and the
Lord Culpepper or either of them or otherwise and all
my Estate right title interest term and terms of years
claims and demand therein whatsoever under the rents
covenants and agreements to be paid and performed to
the Landlord or Landlords thereof according to my
lease thereof   And my Will and mind is that my Executor and Overseers or the greater number of them by
sale of the timber and trees and Underwoods now
growing upon my Woods called or known by the name
or names of Sansome Woods in the Forrest of Sherwood in the county of Nottingham shall levy and raise
the sum of fifteen hundred pounds towards the payment
of my Legacies aforesaid if so much money can be
raised by the sale of the said timber trees and Underwoods or otherwise so much as can be raised by the sale
of the same   And to that purpose I do hereby give and

bequeath all the said timber trees and Underwoods now growing upon the said Woods called Sansome Woods unto the Executor and Overseers of this my Will and free liberty power and authority unto or for them or the survivors or survivor of them or the heirs executors or admors of such survivor or the greater number of them to sell and dispose of the same and thereby to levy and raise the sum of fifteen hundred pounds for the purposes aforesaid or so much as can be raised by such sale and my Will and mind is that the rest and residue of my debts Legacies and funeral expences over and above what shall be raised by the sale of the said Sansome Woods as aforesaid shall be raised paid and discharged out of my personal Estate And as for and concerning all and every the overplus rest and residue of my goods chattels and personal Estate whatsoever not hereinbefore bequeathed or disposed of after the payment and discharge of my funeral charges debts and Legacies I give and bequeath the same unto and amongst all my younger Sons John Jennens Humfrey Jennens Robert Jennens and William Jennens and the survivors and survivor of them equally share and share alike at their respective ages of one and twenty years each Son to have his respective share or part thereof as they shall respectively attain to the said age of one and twenty years And if any of my said younger Sons shall be of the age of one and twenty years or above at my decease then he or they being of such age to have his or their respective share or part thereof within the space of three years next after my decease And if any of my said younger Sons shall depart this natural life without issue before his or their respective ages of one and twenty years then my Will and mind is that the share and part of him or them so dying shall be equally divided amongst the survivors or survivor of my said younger Sons which have attained or shall attain unto the said age of one and twenty years Nevertheless my Will is that there shall not be any distribution of the said Overplus until the end of three years after my decease And because my books here and at Suitterton cannot conveniently be parted or divided I do therefore give all the same unto my Son Charles desiring him to give some part thereof to each of his Brothers such as he shall think proper for them And furthermore I do by this my Will give devise and dispose of the Guardianship and tuition of all my Children which shall be under the age of one and twenty years and of all and every their messuages lands tenements goods and chattels during their respective minorities and until they shall respectively attain unto the respective ages of one and twenty years unto Mary my Wife their dear and loving Mother if she live so long and continue unmarried after my decease And after her decease or remarriage which shall next happen Then I give and dispose of the said Guardianship and Tuition unto and do appoint my Son Charles to be Guardian of all my said younger Children and of their Estate during their respective minorities And I do hereby nominate make and appoint my said Son Charles to be the sole and only Executor of this my last Will and Testament not doubting of his careful just and faithful performance of the same And I do hereby nominate make appoint and desire my trusty and well beloved friends S^r. Charles Holt S^r. Clement Fisher and S^r. John Bridgeman Baronetts and Robert Burdett Esqre. to be the Overseers of this my Will desiring their advice and assistance to my Executor Wife and Children from time to time in the management of their respective Estate and in the execution of this my Will desiring their acceptance of this trouble with the like readiness and good will as I should have done the like for any of them if they or any of them had desired the like from me and I had survived them And for their pains therein I give unto each of them the sum of ten pounds apiece as a token of my love and in remembrance of me their friend And my Will and mind is that if any loss shall happen by disposing of any sum or sums of money or by the deficiency or insolvency of any tenant or tenants debtor or debtors or otherwise without the wilful default or neglect of my Executor or Overseers or any of them that the same loss shall be borne and sustained by and out of my own Estate and that my Executors or Overseers or any of them their or any of their heirs executors or admors or any of them shall not be liable unto or chargeable with the same And that my said Executor and Overseers shall be chargeable and charged with and for his and their own particular actings receipts and disbursements relating to this my Will and not one for the other or for the act receipt disbursement default or neglect of the other of them And my Will and mind is That if any dispute difference or controversy shall arise between my Wife and Children or any of them concerning the managing parting or dividing of my Estate or otherwise relating to this my Will (which I pray God to prevent) then my Will and mind is that the same shall be fully referred unto ended and decided by the Overseers of this my Will or the greater number of them from time to time desiring all my Children upon my blessing to stand to abide and perform their end and determination therein from time to time and to be dutiful to their Mother and loving and respectful one to another   And my Will and mind is   That my Executor and Overseers and every of them shall be allowed all such reasonable charges and expences as they or any of them respectively shall be put unto or sustain in execution and performance of this my Will or anywise relating to the same   And lastly I do hereby revoke and make void all Wills by me formerly made and do declare this to be my last Will and Testament   In Witness whereof I have hereunto put my hand and seal the day and year first above written—HUMFREY JENNENS— Signed Sealed and published by the within named Humfrey Jennens to be his last Will and Testament in the presence of us whose names are subscribed who did all of us subscribe our names as Witnesses—in the Testators presence — J. Holden — Edw Birch — Tho Homer—Jeremiah Bordall.

> " PROBATUM fuit humor Testamtum apud London Decimo Octavo die mensis July Anno Domi Millimo Sexcenmo et nonagemo coram veuli at egregio viro Dn⁰· Thoma Pinfold Milite legum Dcore Surro venlis et egregij viri Dui Richardi Ranies Militis legum etiam Decoris buriœ Progat Cantuar Magri custodis sive Condy

ltime constituti Juramto Caroli Jennens filij dci deft et Extoris vuici in deo Testamto nominat Cui Comissa fuit Admco oium et Singulom bonoru jurium et Creditoru ejusdem Deft de bene et fidelr admstrando eadem ad sancta Dei Evangelia Jurat."

1867. B. No. 110.

IN CHANCERY. Total folios 67.
LORD CHANCELLOR.
VICE-CHANCELLOR JAMES.

Between SAMUEL BAYLIS (deceased) - *Plaintiff*
and
THE HONORABLE MARY
HOWARD and FREDERICK
EARL BEAUCHAMP - - *Defendants*
By Original Bill

AND

Between JAMES BAYLIS - - - *Plaintiff*
and
The said MARY HOWARD and
FREDERICK EARL BEAUCHAMP *Defendants*
By Order of Revivor.

AFFIDAVITS FILED ON THE PART OF THE PLAINTIFF BY MESSRS. GODFREY & CO. OF NO. 6 SOUTH SQUARE GRAY'S INN HIS SOLICITORS.

Filed 12th March 1869.

I WILLIAM JOHNSON of 13 Smith Street in the parish of Saint George's Birmingham gold chain maker make oath and say:

1. I am now 65 years of age and that on the 2d day of August 1824 I intermarried with Sarah Granger at Old Edgbaston Church Birmingham aforesaid the daughter of Sarah Granger who was one of the daughters of Elizabeth Perry The said Elizabeth Perry was one of the daughters of Mary Blyth the testatrix in the pleadings in this cause named and one of the parties entitled to her residuary personal estate.

2. I have always been informed and believe that the will of Mary Blyth was formerly in the possession of Joseph Patrick and was kept by him until his death and that the said will remained in the possession of his widow Mary Patrick who on the decease of her husband Joseph Patrick gave it to her daughter Mary Jennens wife of John White of No. 131 Lee Bank Road Edgbaston Birmingham aforesaid by whom it was given up for the purposes of the above suit to Abraham Ward Rhodes Mary Ann Rhodes William Rhodes and Eliza Rhodes.

                              Sworn at Birmingham in the county of Warwick this 11th day of March 1869

WILLIAM JOHNSON.   Before me

                              W. H. GRIFFITHS

                              A Commissioner to administer

Folios 5.   oaths in Chancery in England.

                              Filed 12th March 1869.

I MARY PATRICK residing in the Licensed Victuallers Asylum Bristol Street Birmingham in the county of Warwick widow of Joseph Patrick of the

185

Licensed Victuallers Asylum Bristol Street aforesaid make oath and say:

1. That the will of my late husband Joseph Patrick and that of Mary Blythe were never out of my possession until they were given up to my daughter Mary Jennens Hales White the wife of John White of No. 131 Lee Bank Road Edgbaston Birmingham in the county of Warwick.

The mark of
X
MARY PATRICK.*

Folios 4.

Sworn at Birmingham in the county of Warwick this 11th day of March 1869 this affidavit having been previously read over by me to the deponent who seemed perfectly to understand the same and made her mark thereto in my presence
W. H. GRIFFITHS
A Commissioner to administer oaths in Chancery in England.

Filed 12th March 1869.

I JOHN BROOKE PERREN of No. 17 Metcalf Place Pentonville Road in the Parish of Clerkenwell in the county of Middlesex formerly traveller to an oil and colourman but now out of business make oath and say as follows:

1. I am 59 years of age and that on the 8th day of May 1832 I intermarried with Caroline the daughter of

*The correspondence between Mrs. Patrick and Lady Andover is dated 1800. Deponent must now have been nearly 90 years of age, and too infirm to sign her name.

John William Mencke and Fanny his wife formerly residing rear Finsbury Square in the county of Middlesex bankers clerk.

2. The said Fanny Mencke was one of the children of John and Sarah Elgar of Lambourne in the county of Berks The said Fanny Mencke was a cousin of Sarah Heath wife of Joseph Heath of Welford in the county of Berks aforesaid farmer.

3. The said Sarah Heath was one of the children of Joseph Ambrose of Maidencourt Farm East Garston Berkshire aforesaid.

4. About 30 years since as near as I can recollect I was either reading from a newspaper or hearing it read at Inkpen Cottage Croyden Common in the county of Surrey the residence of the said Fanny Mencke and where I then resided a statement of large property belonging to a family of the name of Jennens which property was described in the said newspaper as of fabulous amount The said Fanny Mencke repeating the name of Jennens several times said Jennens is the name of a very rich man who married one of the Ambrose's daughters of East Garston Berkshire.

5. And I further make oath that she has often repeated the same statement in my hearing and she has often since that time spoken of it as having heard of such marriage from her relations when she was young.

6. I have deposed to the foregoing facts contained in this my affidavit from my intimate acquaintances with most of the parties named and I have deposed to

such facts according to the best and utmost of my knowledge remembrance information and belief.

JOHN BROOKE PERREN.

Folios 6.

Sworn at the Record and Writ Clerk's Office Chancery Lane in the county of Middlesex this 11th day of March 1869.
Before me
E. GRUBB.

Filed 12th March 1869.

I FRANCIS WELLINGTON MOORE of Duffield in the county of Derby clerk make oath and say:

1. That I am the vicar of Duffield aforesaid and have been so since the year 1858.

2. That some time in the year 1860 applications were made to me by some persons for certificates supposed to be in my custody referring to the pedigree of the Jennens family I on or about the 4th day of May 1860 caused an advertisement to be inserted in the Derby and Chesterfield Reporter and which advertisement I believe was in the words and figures following " Applications having been made some time since for " registers connected with the Jennens family notice is " given that registers have lately been found in the old " vicarage house of Duffield of the existence of which " the vicar was not aware Parties who are interested " in the above property may be glad to know this " Apply to the Revd. F. W. Moore Duffield Derby."

3. That the said registers or documents purporting to be registers were so discovered by the late Miss Ward

sister of Thomas Ward esquire whose father was formerly vicar of Duffield and handed to me this deponent by the said Miss Ward in the presence of the said Thomas Ward as well as some loose papers of entries of baptisms and burials at Belper and Turnditch in the said county of Derby.

4. That the certificate of baptism now produced and shewn to me marked with the letter "A" is one of the certificates copied from the register of baptisms for the parish of Duffield in the county of Derby.

FRANCIS W. MOORE.

Folios 6.

Sworn at Derby in the county of Derby this 10th day of March 1869
Before me
WM. BOROUGH.
A Commissioner to administer oaths in Chancery in England.

Filed 12th March 1869.

I ELIZA RHODES the wife of William Rhodes of Bodesley in the borough of Birmingham in the county of Warwick make oath and say:

1. I am now 61 years of age and that I with my mother and grandmother Elizabeth Perry hereinafter named were many years ago residing together in the same house in Hartford Street Hockley Birmingham in the county of Warwick.

2. That during the time we so resided together as aforesaid I have frequently and from time to time heard my said grandmother Elizabeth the wife of Isaac Perry

deceased (who was the daughter of the late John and Mary Blyth deceased in the said pleadings named and granddaughter of the late James and Mary Essex whose maiden name was Mary Jennens and great granddaughter of the late John Jennens gentleman deceased these last-named parties being also in the said pleadings severally named) say that her mother the said Mary Blyth used to state that her grandmother Mary Essex then Mary Jennens spinster was just before her mariage with the said James Essex residing with her father the said John Jennens (who in the said pleadings is also called John Jennens the grandson) of Dudderston Hall in the county of Warwick aforesaid and that the said Mary Jennens did without the consent of her father the said John Jennens and against his wish quit his house and marry the said James Essex and that such conduct on the part of the said Mary Jennens afterwards Mary Essex was the sole cause of the said John Jennens quitting Dudderston Hall to reside in some other part of the kingdom and that the said Mary Essex did after her said marriage reside with her said husband at Saltley Hall in the said county of Warwick until the time of his death which took place in the year 1721 having had by his said wife Mary four children and no more who survived him that is to say John Essex James Essex Ann Essex and her grandmother the before mentioned Mary Essex afterwards the wife of the said John Blyth and my great-grandmother.

The said Mary Essex some time after the death of her first husband married with one John Handy from which marriage there was issue one child only a son who died in his infancy.

4. The said John Handy being a person of profligate habits soon reduced his said wife and her before-mentioned children by her first marriage from a condition of elegance and comfort to one of narrow circumstances.

5. I have heard my grandmother the before-named Elizabeth Perry say and I verily believe it to be true that her mother the said Mary Blyth was generally admitted to be and she herself was well aware of the fact that she was a cousin to the late William Jennens deceased of Acton the intestate in the pleadings in this cause named but she the said Mary Blyth was so far advanced in years and in such indigent circumstances at the death of the said William Jennens that she was unable to prosecute her claim against the estates of the said William Jennens and that she intrusted the prosecution of her rights and interests therein to the care of her son-in-law one Thomas Patrick.

6. The said Thomas Patrick accordingly undertook to prosecute the claims of the said Mary Blyth and also those of her family against the estate of the said William Jennens and accordingly he proceeded to search the churches in and about Birmingham and other parts of the country for registers relating to the baptisms marriages and deaths of their ancestors and other documents and also other evidence tending to prove the connection between the said William Jennens and the said Mary Blyth.

7. The said Thomas Patrick having obtained an accurate pedigree of the said family by means of such his exertions on behalf of the said Mary Blyth as aforesaid the wife of the said Thomas Patrick wrote several letters upon the subject to Lady Andover in the said pleadings named and also to other persons having or claiming to be connected with the said family of the Jennens but that at this time the said Thomas Patrick suddenly broke off all farther enquiries and ceased to interfere in the interests of the said Mary Blyth with respect to the property of the said William Jennens or the claims of any other person therein without assigning any reason for his conduct in so doing.

8. The said Thomas Patrick never disclosed to anyone the reason why he had thus abandoned any further investigation of the affair but that at that time he was known to have suddenly become a rich man from a state of comparative poverty and having portioned off his family he passed the rest of his life in seclusion.

9. I further say that about the year 1830 two gentlemen met me in the yard attached to the beforementioned house in Harford Street aforesaid who asked me to introduce them to my grandmother the said Elizabeth Perry as they were anxious to see her for the purpose of gaining her consent for them to cut through the said Duddestone estate in the county of Warwick so far as her interest therein as a descendant of the said John Jennens of Duddestone Hall aforesaid was concerned. I accordingly introduced them to my said

grandmother the said Elizabeth Perry and I verily believe that at that interview with the said two gentlemen she did give such consent as aforesaid.

10. I further say that I have heard my said grandmother the said Elizabeth Perry state that her mother the said Mary Blyth received a watercourse rental from one Mrs. Hall who lived at the sign of the Bell Inn Philips Street Birmingham aforesaid which property was known by the name of Ashford Croft leading from High Street New Street to Worcester Street and down to Philips Street and once in the possession of the said John Jennens of Dudderstone Hall in the county of Warwick aforesaid.

11. I am enabled to depose to the foregoing facts contained in this my affidavit from family relatives and their connection respecting the intestate William Jennens in the pleadings in this cause named also from my personal knowledge of and my acquaintance with several of the persons herein-before named including my said grandmother and mother and I have deposed to such facts accordingly to the best and utmost of my knowledge information remembrance and belief.

Eliza Rhodes.

Folios 17.

Sworn at Birmingham in the county of Warwick this 11th day of March 1869.
Before me
H. W. Griffiths
A Commissioner to administer oaths in Chancery in England.

Filed 12th March 1869.

We ABRAHAM WARD RHODES of 188 Alderley Street Birmingham in the county of Warwick fire-iron maker MARY ANN RHODES of Birmingham aforesaid wife of the said Abraham Ward Rhodes WILLIAM RHODES of Sandy Lane Birmingham aforesaid fire-iron maker and ELIZA RHODES wife of the said William Rhodes jointly and severally make oath and say:

And I first the said Abraham Ward Rhodes for myself say:

1. I am one of the children of John Rhodes late of Birmingham in the county of Warwick fire iron maker and Elizabeth Rhodes his wife On the 3d day of September 1838 I intermarried with my second cousin the deponent Mary Ann Rhodes formerly Mary Ann Asprey.

And I the said Mary Ann Rhodes for myself say:

2. I am one of the children of William Asprey of Oxford Street Birmingham in the county of Warwick gilt toy maker and Mary his wife and a granddaughter of Ann Asprey wife of Thomas Asprey of Moland Street Birmingham in the county of Warwick gilt button maker The said Ann Asprey was one of the children of Sarah Bannister the wife of George Bannister of Philip Street Birmingham in the county of Warwick button burnisher The said Sarah Bannister was one of the children of Mary Blythe the testatrix in the pleadings in this cause mentioned.

O

And I the said William Rhodes for myself say :

3. That I am the brother of the deponent Abraham Ward Rhodes being one of the children of the said John Rhodes.

4. On the 13th of December 1840 I intermarried with my cousin the deponent Eliza Rhodes.

And I the said Eliza Rhodes for myself say:

5. That I am the only child of Joseph Biggs of Birmingham in the county of Warwick cabinet maker and Mary his wife That the said Mary Biggs was one of the children of Elizabeth Perry the wife of Issac Perry of Birmingham in the county of Warwick stamper and tool maker and that the said Elizabeth Perry was one of the children of the said Mary Blythe the testatrix in the pleadings in this cause mentioned.

6. That we the said Abraham Ward Rhodes Mary Ann Rhodes William Rhodes and Eliza Rhodes jointly and severally say as follows :

7. We believe the said William Jennens the intestate in the pleadings in this cause mentioned was the only child of Robert Jennens in the bill of complaint in this cause called Robert Jennens the younger formerly of the parish of St. Andrew Holborn in the county of Middlesex and Anne his wife both of whom died in his lifetime and that neither of them the said Robert Jennens and Anne his wife had any issue except the said William Jennens the intestate in the pleadings in this cause mentioned.

8. We believe that the said Robert Jennens the younger was one of the two children of Robert Jennens

late of Reading in the county of Berkshire (hereinafter called Robert Jennens the elder) who respectively were named Martha Jennens and Robert Jennens.

9. We believe that the said Robert Jennens the elder died in the year 1683 a widower leaving his son the said Robert Jennens the younger his only child him surviving.*

10. We believe that the said Robert Jennens the younger was baptized on the 18th day of June 1672 and that he is the same person that is named and described in the certificate of baptism now produced and shewn to me at the time of making this our affidavit and marked with the letter A.

11. We believe that the said Robert Jennens intermarried with Ann Guidott on the 17th of October 1700 at Westminster in the county of Middlesex and that the said Robert Jennens the younger and Ann Guidott are respectively the Robert Jennens and Ann Guidott referred to in the certificate of marriage now produced and shewn to us at the time of making this our affidavit and marked with the letter B.

12. We believe that the said Robert Jennens the younger died on the 25th day of February 1726 at Bedford Row in the parish of St. Andrew's Holborn in the county of Middlesex and that he was buried at Acton in the county of Suffolk.

---

*When William Lygon applied for letters of administration *de bonis non* of Robert Jennens, the father of William Jennens the intestate, he described the said Robert as a widower. That evidently was a mistake. Was he thinking of William's grandfather, Robert the elder?

13. We believe the said Robert Jennens the elder was baptised on the 9th day of July 1644 at Duffield in the county of Derby and that he is the same person who is named and described in the certificate of baptism now produced and shewn to us at the time of making this our affidavit and marked with the letter "C."

14. We believe the said Robert Jennens the elder was one of the sons of John Jennens (herein-after called John Jennens the son) who was one of the seven children of John Jennens of Birmingham aforesaid ironmonger who died in the year 1653 and who were respectively named the said John Jennens the son, Abraham Jennens, Humphrey Jennens, Joseph Jennens, Edward Jennens, Sarah Jennens, and Hester Jennens.

15. We believe the said John Jennens the son was baptised on the 8th day of March 1607 in the parish church of St. Martin Birmingham aforesaid and that he is the same person who is named and described in the certificate of baptism now produced and shewn to us at the time of making this our affidavit and marked with the letter D.

16. We believe that on the 15th day of May 1636 he intermarried with Jane Ambrose formerly of East Garston in the county of Berks at East Garston Church We believe that the said John Jennens and Jane Ambrose are respectively the same parties who are named and described in the declaration now produced and shown to us at the time of making this our affidavit and marked with the letter E.

17. We believe that the said John Jennens and Jane his wife subsequently to their marriage removed to

Birmingham aforesaid and that the said John Jennens died in or about the year 1650 and was buried at Birmingham aforesaid* That there were issue of the said John Jennens and Jane Ambrose five children and no more (that is to say) Jane Jennens (who was never married) John Jennens (hereinafter called the said John Jennens the grandson) William Jennens, the said Robert Jennens, (the grandfather of the said William Jennens the intestate) and Roger Jennens, all of whom died in the lifetime of the said William Jennens the intestate.

18. We believe the said John Jennens the grandson was baptised on the 19th April 1640 in the said parish church of St. Martin's Birmingham aforesaid and that he is the person who is named and described in the certificate of baptism now produced and shewn to us at the time of making this our affidavit and marked with the letter " D."

19. We believe that the said John Jennens intermarried with Dorothy Bridgins in the said parish church of St. Martin's Birmingham aforesaid and that the said John Jennens and Dorothy Bridgins are respectively the same persons who are named and described in the certificate of marriage now produced and shewn to us at the time of making this our affidavit and marked with the letter " E."

20. We believe that the said John Jennens was buried on the 11th of November 1710 and that he is the same person who is named and described in the certificate of burial now produced and shewn to us at the

* This is a mistake. The Deponents had perused the Will of John Jennens, who died in 1653, and concluded that his son John was then dead.

time of making this our affidavit and marked with the letter " F."

21. We believe that there was issue of the said John Jennens and Dorothy Jennens his wife one child and no more namely Mary Jennens who died in the lifetime of the said William Jennens the intestate having intermarried first with James Essex and secondly with John Handy and having had issue five children and no more namely by her said first husband Ann Essex, John Essex, Mary Essex, James Essex, and by her said second husband William Handy all of whom except the said Mary Essex died in the lifetime of the said William Jennens the intestate and without having been married.

22. The said William Jennens the son of the said John Jennens the son had issue three children and no more namely William Jennens, Louis Jennens, and Edward Jennens, all of whom died in the lifetime of the said William Jennens the intestate.

23. The said Roger Jennens had issue three children and no more namely Jacob Jennens, Joseph Jennens, and Anne Jennens, all of whom died in the lifetime of the said William Jennens the intestate.

24. We believe that the said Mary Essex intermarried with John Blythe and died a widow on the 3d day of July 1799 having survived the said William Jennens the intestate and having duly made and signed her last will and testament in writing bearing date the 29th day of June 1799 being the will referred to in the pleadings in this cause mentioned The same Mary Blythe is the same person who is named and described in the certificate of burial now produced and shewn to

us at the time of swearing this our affidavit and marked with the letter G.

25. And we the said Abraham Ward Rhodes, Mary Ann Rhodes, William Rhodes, and Eliza Rhodes, jointly and severally say:

26. We have deposed to the foregoing facts contained in this our affidavit from family relations and other connections respecting the said intestate William Jennens also from our personal knowledge of and acquaintance with some of the parties hereinbefore named and also from a perusal of the entries in the family Bible* and other books hereinbefore referred to and from a perusal of the will of John Jennens of Birmingham aforesaid hereinbefore called John Jennens the elder proved in the Prerogative Court of Canterbury on the 10th day of March 1653 And we have deposed to the foregoing facts to the best of our knowledge information and belief

ABRAHAM WARD RHODES.
MARY ANN RHODES.
WILLIAM RHODES.
ELIZA RHODES.

Sworn by the deponents Abraham Ward Rhodes Mary Ann Rhodes William Rhodes and Eliza Rhodes at Birmingham in the county of Warwick this 11th day of March 1869
Before me
H. W. GRIFFITHS
A Commissioner to administer oaths
Folios 25. in Chancery in England.

---
* The Family Bible hereinbefore referred to.

Filed 12th March 1869.
I JAMES BAYLIS of Fulford Barracks Canterbury in the county of Kent farrier serjeant make oath and say as follows:

1. I am about 40 years of age and am the son of Samuel Baylis who was the grandson of Mary Blythe the testatrix in this cause mentioned.

2. I have heard my grandfather and grandmother say that Mary Blythe was second cousin to William Jennens of Acton in the county of Suffolk esquire the intestate in the pleadings in this cause named and that he was the great grandson of John Jennens the younger of Birmingham whose father and grandfather had property in Sutton Courtenay in the county of Berks.

JAMES BAYLIS.

Sworn at the city of Canterbury the 10th day of March 1869
Before me
J. WILKINSON
A Commissioner to administer oaths in Chancery in England.

Folios 4.

EXTRACTED from the District Registry of Her Majesty's Court of Probate at Lichfield.

" (In the Bishop's Court at Lichfield.)

" IN THE NAME OF GOD AMEN I JOHN JENNENS of the parish of Aston juxta Birmingham and County of Warwick Mason being in perfect mind and understanding praised be God for the same do for the settling of my Estate make this my last Will and Testament

in manner following Imprimis I wish that my debts
and funeral charges be first paid and satisfied Item I
give to my daughter Mary Jennings her Heirs Executors
Administrators and Assigns for ever all my Estates
both real and personal and I make her the said MARY
JENNINGS EXECUTRIX hereof revoking all Wills by me
heretofore made IN WITNESS whereof I have hereunto put my Hand and Seal this 18th day of March in
the 1st year of the Reign of our Sovereign Lady Anne
now Queene of England Anne Dom. 1702.

" SIGNED sealed and published
the day and year above written
by the said John Jennens as
and for his last Will and } JOHN JENNENS.
Testament in the presence of
us who have subscribed our
Names as Witnesses (L.S.)

   " Thos Bleu
   " Edwd Hares
   " Henry Hedley
     " Proved by Oath of Mary Essex
     otherwise Jennings.
       " Sworn under £20.
" Exd 16th June 1852."

  EXTRACTED from the Principal Registry of
   Her Majesty's Court of Probate.
" (In the Prerogative Court of Canterbury.)
 " THIS IS THE LAST WILL and TESTAMENT of me
MARY HOWARD commonly called VISCOUNTESS ANDOVER

I leave my daughter the Honble Francess Howard sole Executrix and Residuary Legatee of all my personal Estate after the payment of all my debts & funeral expences and such legacies as I shall mention in this my Will or any Codicil annexed to it and it is also my Will and desire that any Box Letter or Parcel directed by me as a Remembrance to any friend may be dilivered to them I do most earnestly will and desire that all moneys justly due from me to my eldest daughter the Honble Catherine Howard as may be seen by her Accounts kept by me may be so secured and made the most of for her that with the friendship and advise of her Sister M$^{rs.}$ Howard & her good brother in law M$^{r.}$ Howard she may never want any of the comforts & necessarys of life that she is capable of enjoying I will and bequeath to my said daughter Catherine Howard my Gold Watch made by Thompston it was her Fathers watch & I hope she will receive it as a kind remembrance from us both I will and bequeath to my daughter Frances Howard all portrate pictures & plate belonging to me at the time of my death the latter (viz$^{t.}$) the plate nevertheless subject to my debts & the discharge of this my Will in case I do not leave money sufficient to pay them I leave to my dear daughter Charlotte Countess Dow$^{r.}$ of Suffolk my Gold Repeating Watch made by Graham with all the seals & lockets anex'd to it I leave to all my Servants that live with me at Elford at the time of my death a years wages over and above what may be owing to them at the time of my death and I leave Eight hundred pounds to be equaly divided between my four old Servants W^m. Giles Frances Mandy Sophia Weston and John Edwards in case they live with me at the time of my death I leave to the poor of the parish of Elford Five hundred pounds to be disposed of to or for them by my Executrix in whatever manner she may judge may be most advantagious for them I desire to be buried in the Vaul with my husband Lord Andover in the Church Yard at Elford and in the most decent and private manner possible attended only by my good Tennants and Servants and I will to have a Leaden Coffin This is my last Will and Testament revoking every former Will or Wills I have ever made and to which I set my hand and seal this twentith day of March 1795——MARY ANDOVER (L.S.) ——Witness—Clementina Maria Elizabetha Sawrey John Sneyd."

"On M^r. W^m. Jennins death a great personal comes to me he died the 19th June 1798 and least I should die before I could make another more enlarged Will I leave a Codicil annexed to this by me—MARY ANDOVER—

" 5th April 1803.

"ON WHICH DAY APPEARED PERSONALLY RICHARD HOWARD of the parish of Saint George Hanover Square in the County of Middlesex Esquire and made Oath that he is the lawful husband of The Honorable Frances Howard the natural and lawful daughter and sole Executrix named in the last Will and Testament of The Right Honorable Mary Howard commonly called Viscountess Andover late of Elford in the County of

Stafford Widow deceased and which said Will is now
hereunto annexed bearing date the twentieth day of
March 1795 and this Deponent saith that on a day
happening in the month of May 1801 he this Deponent
being with the said deceased at her house at Elford
aforesaid she the said deceased did produce to this
Deponent her said Will which had then a Codicil
annexed thereto wherein she had bequeathed a Legacy
of Ten thousand pounds to The Reverend Mr. John
Sneyd but wherein was contained no other legacy whatever and that the said deceased did then in this Deponents presence cancel the said Codicil by tearing the
same and desiring the Deponent to put it in the fire
which he did in her presence and this Deponent well
knows that she the said deceased did so in consequence
of her having previously given the said sum of Ten
thousand pounds to the said Reverend Mr. John Sneyd
and this Deponent lastly saith that since the death of
the said deceased this Deponent hath diligently
searched amongst the deceased's papers and writings
of consequence and is in his consience assured and
convinced that the said Will hereunto annexed is the
last Will and Testament of the said deceased and that
she the said deceased hath not left behind her any
Codicil whatever thereto——RICHARD HOWARD—Same
day the said Richard Howard was duly sworn to the
truth of this Affidavit before me—J. SEWELL Surr.—
Pres^{t.} GEO. BOGG Not. Pub^{c.}

" PROVED at London 5th April 1803 before the Worshipful James Henry Arnold Doctor of Laws and

Surrogate by the Oath of the Honorable Frances (by mistake in the Will written Francess) Howard (Wife of Richard Howard Esquire) the daughter the sole Executrix to whom administration was granted having been first sworn duly to administer."

"On the 12th July 1827. Administration of the Goods Chattels and Credits of The Right Honorable Lady Mary Howard commonly called Viscountess Andover Widow deceased left unadministered by the Honorable Frances Howard (Wife of Richard Howard Esquire) deceased whilst living the daughter sole Executrix and Residuary Legatee was granted to The Right Honorable Heneage Earl of Aylesford the sole Executor and Residuary Legatee named in the Will and Codicils of the Right Honorable Heneage Earl of Aylesford who was the sole Executor and Residuary Legatee named in the Will of Heneage heretofore Earl of Aylesford limited to the sum of One thousand one hundred and forty six pounds thirteen shillings and three pence Stock Old South Sea Annuities standing in the name of the said Lady Mary Howard and to all interest and dividends due and to grow due thereon but no further or otherwise or in any other manner whatsoever having been first sworn duly to administer William Bagot Esquire the Administrator (with the Will annexed) of the Goods unadministered of the said Honorable Frances Howard (Wife of Richard Howard deceased) having been first duly cited with the usual Intimation but in no wise appeared (as by Acts of Court appears)."

On the 24th December, 1831 Administration of the Goods Chattels and Credits of The Right Honorable Mary Howard commonly called Viscountess Andover late of Elford in the County of Stafford Widow deceased left unadministered by the Honorable Frances Howard (Wife of Richard Howard Esquire) deceased whilst living the daughter sole Executrix and Residuary Legatee named in the said Will was granted to James Hillen of Bloxhall in the County of Suffolk Land Valuer as a person for that purpose named by and on the part and behalf of Susannah Andrews of Harbourne in the County of Stafford Widow limited for the purpose only of attending supplying substantiating and confirming the proceedings already had or that shall or may hereafter be had in a certain cause or Suit in the High Court of Chancery between William Andrews and the said Susannah Andrews then the Wife of the said William Andrews and The Right Honorable Katharine Countess of Beauchamp Widow and William Bagot Esquire or in any other Cause or Suit which may hereafter be commenced in the same or any other Court between the aforesaid parties or any other parties touching or concerning the premises and until a final Decree shall be had and made therein and the said Decree carried into execution and the Execution thereof fully completed but no further or otherwise or in any other manner whatsoever having been first sworn (by Commission) duly to administer The said William Bagot Esquire one of the Executors of the Will of Richard Howard deceased whilst living the lawful husband Executor according to the tenor of and sole person entitled to the Effects of the Honorable Frances Howard deceased whilst living the daughter sole Executrix and Residuary Legatee named in the said Will as aforesaid having been first duly cited with the usual Intimation but in no wise appeared (as by Acts of Court appears).

On the 13th April 1863 Letters of Administration with the Will annexed of the rest of the personal Estate and Effects of The Right Honorable Mary Howard commonly called Viscountess Andover late of Elford in the County of Stafford Widow deceased who died on the 7th March 1803 at Elford aforesaid left unadministered by The Honorable Frances (in the Will written Francess) Howard Wife of Richard Howard Esquire deceased whilst living the daughter of the said deceased and the sole Executrix and Residuary Legatee named in the said Will were granted to The Honorable Mary Howard Widow the Administratrix with the Will of all and singular the personal Estate and Effects twice left unadministered of the said Honorable Frances Howard deceased she having been first sworn duly to administer.

Extracted from the District Registry of Her Majesty's Court of Probate at Lichfield.

" (In the Bishop's Court of Lichfield.)

"On the eleventh day of April 1712 Letters of Administration of all and singular the personal Estate and Effects of Roger Ganney late of the parish of Duffield in the County of Derby were granted by the Bishop's Court of Lichfield to Isabella Ganney the lawful Widow and Relict of the deceased she having been first sworn duly to administer.

"Effects under 5£"

Extracted from the Principal Registry of Her Majesty's Court of Probate.
"In the Prerogative Court of Canterbury.
"March, 1762.

"ANN JENNENS On the tenth day Administration of the Goods Chattels and Credits of Ann Jennens late of the Parish of St George Hanover Square in the County of Middlesex Widow deceased was granted to William Jennens Esquire the natural and lawful Son of the said deceased having been first sworn duly to administer. Admon of Goods unadministered in July 1798."

EXTRACTED from the Principal Registry of Her Majesty's Court of Probate.
"In the Prerogative Court of Canterbury.

"IN THE NAME OF GOD AMEN the eight and twentieth daie of Maye Anno Dni 1625 And in the ffirst yeare of the Raigne of our Soveraigne Lord Charles by the grace of god Kinge of England Scotland France and Ireland Defender of the faith &c. I AMBROSE JENNENS Cittizen and Cordwaynor of London beinge att this present sicke in bodie but yet of good and perfecte minde and remembrance laud and praise I therefore give unto Allmightie god and consideringe with myself the mutabilitie of this life and the certentie of Death although the tyme and hower thereof be altogeather uncertaine and to thend and intente to be the better prepared and settled in minde whensoever it shall please the Lord to take me out of this transitory life I doe therefore by godes permission make and declare this my presente Testamente wherein is conteyned my laste will in manner and forme followeinge (that is to saie) First and above all things I doe commend my soule into the handes of Almightee God my Maker hopeinge and assuredlie beleevinge by and through the precious death passion and resurrecon of Jesus Christ his Sonne my onlie Saviour and redeemer to be saved and to have free pardon and forgivenes of all my sinnes and iniquities and everlastinge life in the kingdome of heaven amongst the electe And my bodie I committ to the earth to be buried in such Christian seemely and decent sorte and manner as to the good discretion of Hester my lovinge wife shall be thought fitt and I doe make ordaine and constitute her the said Hester my Wife my full and sole executrix of this my present testamente and last Will wherein I doubte not but shee will take speciall care and regard by good advice of frendes and otherwaies to see the same performed in all thinges accordinge to my true meaninge here in after expressed and declared and becaus there shall not be anie question made of or againste this my will I doe

P

therefore revoke disanull and make void all former willes legacies and bequests by me heretofore made or given and this to stande and abide for and as my laste will and non other and as touchinge the disposinge of all such goodes chattells Leases wares merchandizes plate moveables houshold stuffe and other my personall estate and things wherewith it hath pleased the Lord to bless and endew me withall or that to me shall be due cominge or belonginge or that ought to come accrew or belonginge unto me att the tyme of my decease by anie waies or meanes right title interest contracte bargaine or agreemente whatsoever or otherwise howsoever I doe will give devise and dispose of the same in manner and forme followeing (that is to saie) And my minde and will is that within convenient tyme after my decease my goodes chattelles leases plate moveables household stuffe and other my personall estate be uprightlie and indifferentlie prized and valued accordinge to the laudable custome and usage of and within the cittee of London and that my debtes beinge thereout first taken and deducted which my will is shall be paid and satisfied or order taken for the paymente of them by my said Executrix within conveniente tyme nexte after my decease I doe give will leave devise and bequeath all my said goodes chattelles leases and other my personall estate in this manner and forme enseuinge (viz.!) one full third parte whereof I doe give and leave unto the said Hester my Wife as to her belongeth by the custome of the Cittie of London another third parte thereof I doe give and leave unto

and amongst all my Children equallie betweene them
and the survivors of them to be parted and divided
accordinge to the custome of the said cittie wherein my
will and desire is that those my Children which are not
yet preferred shall be considered and respected
accordinglie and non of my Children to have greater
parte or share of or in that third parte then another
howsoever some of them have alreadie had greater or
lesser parte or porcon in prefermente of marriage one
then another And thother third parte beinge in myne
owne power to give and dispose of I doe reserve to paie
and satisfie such quitts and legacies as I doe hereafter
will give lymitt and appointe wherein for the presente
as I have considered and thought upon theise hereafter doe followe (viz.!) Item I doe will and give to
Fiftie and seven poore men such as my Executrix
shall thinke good blacke to make everie of them a
Gowne to be worne by them on the daie of my funerall
of such price as shee shall thinke reasonable and
my minde and will is that my said Wife and Executrix
shall for herself and my Children and such other
my frendes as shee shall thinke good have such conveniente blacks as shall be fittinge for which and
for other the charge of and concerninge my funerall
I doe give lymitt and appointe unto her the some of
Two hundred poundes in money to doe and performe
the same withall Item I doe give and bequeath unto
my Sonne William Jennens the some of Five hundred
poundes of lawfull money of England to be paid unto
him att his age of Twentie and one yeares Item I doe

give and bequeathe unto my Sonn Ambrose Jennens the sum of Five hundred poundes of like lawfull money of England to be paid unto him att his age of twenty and one yeares Item I doe give and bequeath unto my Daughter Susan Jennens the some of Five hundred poundes of like money to be paid unto her when shee shall accomplish her full age of twentie and one yeares or be married first happeninge Item I do give and bequeath unto my Daughter Sara Jennens the Lease which I have and hould of certen messuage tenementes groundes and other thinges with their and every of their apptennes scituatte lyeinge and beinge within the precincte of S$^{t.}$ Katherens neere the Tower of London and all my Estate interest and terme to come of in or to the same lease and the said messuage tenementes and premisses therein menconed and which I hold and enioy by vertue of the same lease and my minde and will is that the said porcons and legacies given unto the said William Ambrose and Susan Jennens as aforesaid and the rents and proffitts of the said Lease messuages tenementes and premisses in S$^{t.}$ Katherens given unto my said Daughter Sara shall be kepte imployed and disposed of to and for the benefitt and behoofe of them my said Foure children respectively by the said Hester my Wife to whose care I leave and committ the same And if anie of them my said foure Children shall happen to dye or decease this present lifelong the said William and Ambrose Jennens before they or either of them shall accomplish the full age of Twentie and one yeares respectively And the said Susan and Sara Jennens

before they or either of them shall respectively accomplish the full age of Twentie and one yeares or be
married then my minde and will is that the parte and
porcon of such and soe manie of them as shall soe
happen to dye or decease shall goe and remayne unto
and amongst the survivors or survivor of them my said
Foure Children equallie to be parted and divided wherein
I doe expresse and declare my minde and will further
to be that if the said Sara my daughter shall happen
to dye or decease before shee shall attaine unto her full
age of twentie and one yeares or be married then the
said lease of the said messuage tenementes and premisses with their apptennces in St. Katherens shall be
and remayne unto my said Wife Hester Jennens to and
for her owne use and behoofe and that shee shall in
lieu and recompence thereof paie and allowe unto my
said other three Children William Ambrose and Susan
and the survivors or survivor of them soe much money
as the said lease shall be pryzed att in and by the
Inventarie which shall be taken of my goodes and personall Estate after my decease the same to be equallie
parted and divided betweene and amongst them my
said three Children and the survivors or survivor of
them any thinge aforesaid to the contrarie thereof
in anie wise notwithstandinge I doe give and bequeath
unto my Daughter Marie Garrad the some of One hundred poundes of lawfull money of England Item I give
and bequeathe unto my Daughter Johan Langley the
some of Fiftie poundes of like moneye Item I doe give
and bequeathe unto Susan Langley my grandchilde

daughter of the said Johan Langley the some of fiftie poundes of lawfull English moneye to be paid unto the said Susan att her age of Twentie and one yeares or daie of marriage first happeninge Item I doe give and bequeathe unto my two grand children Marie and Katheren Letherland children of my Daughter Hester the some of One hundred poundes of lawfull money of England (viz$^{t.}$) to either of them fiftie poundes thereof a peece to be paid unto them severallie and respectively accordinge as they shall severally attaine unto and accomplish the full age of twentie and one yeares or be married first happeninge respectively and if either of them the said two children Marie and Katherine shall happen to dye before then I will and give the parte and porcon of such of them as shall soe decease unto the other of them that shall survive Item I do give and bequeathe unto my lovinge Brother Abraham Jennens of plymouth the sume of Fiftie poundes of lawfull money of England the same to be paid and allowed unto him when he shall have made and given a inst and true accompte and recconinge unto my said Executrix of for and concerninge all matters dealinges and businesses in copartnershipp and trade betweene him and me of whose honestie and uprighte dealinge therein I make noe doubte or question of but in regard my greatest estate and means resteth and remayneth in ioynt Trade dealinge and copartnershipp betweene him and me whereby to helpe and maintaine my Wife and Children and to raise them porcons that he will have and take a brotherly love and care in.

performance thereof as I have ever tendered and
loved him and as my truste and confidence is he will
Item I doe give and bequeathe unto my Cozen and
Godsonne Ambrose Jennins Sonn of my said brother
Abraham Jennyns the Some of Thirtie poundes of lawfull english money & to everie one of my said brother
Abrahams other children the some of Twentie poundes
of like money a peece so manie of which said legacies
given to anie of my said Brothers Childeren that be
not of full age or married to be paid unto them severallie
and respectively accordinge as they shall severally
attaine unto and accomplish the full age of Twentie
and one yeares or be married first happeninge respectively Item I doe give and bequeathe unto my
lovinge brother John Jennynes the some of Twentie
poundes of lawfull English money Item I doe give
and bequeath unto my Cozen and Godsonne Ambrose
Jennens Sonne of my said Brother John the some of
Thirtie poundes of lawfull English Moneye and to every
one of my said brother Johns other Children the some
of Twentie poundes of like money a peece soe manie
of which said legacies as are given to anie of my said
Brother Johns Childeren that be not of full age or
married to be paid unto them severally and respectively
accordinge as they shall severally attaine unto and
accomplish the full age of Twentie and one yeares or
be married first happeninge respectively Item I do
give and bequeath unto my Sister Anne Knight the
some of Tenn poundes in money Also I doe give unto
my Cozen Thomas Piddocke Sonne of the said Anne

Knight the like some of tenn poundes in money   Item
I doe give unto my two Cozens Johan and Marie
Jennens Daughters of my eldest Brother Thomas
Jennens deceased to either of them the some of Sixe
poundes Thirteene shillinges and forepence in money a
peece   And if either of them be dead or not livinge att
the tyme of my decease then I give the whole Twentie
markes in money as both the Legacies amounte unto
to such of them as shall be livinge att my decease
Item I doe give unto my Sister Marie Stoner the some
of five poundes in money also I doe give unto the said
Marie Stoners Two Sonnes (viz$^{t.}$) Thomas and John
Stoner Tenn poundes in moneye to be equally parted
and divided by five pounds thereof a peece and to be
paid unto them respectively as they shall severallie
accomplish and come to the full age of twentie and
one yeares and if either of them happen in the meane
tyme to dye then the survivor to have the parte of him
that soe dyeth   Item I doe give unto my good frend
M$^{r.}$ Dunn Parson of S$^{t.}$ Kennett Grace Church blacke
cloth to make him a mourning gowne or Five poundes
in money in liew thereof   Item I doe give to the poore
of the said parish of S$^{t.}$ Kennett Grace Church where
I dwell the some of fourtie shillinges in money to be distributed where most neede shall be   Item I doe give
unto the Masters of the Hospitall of Bridewell the
some of Tenn pounds in money to make them a Repast
or Dinner on the daie of my funerall   Also I doe give
and bequeathe unto the poore Children of the said
Hospitall of Bridewell the some of tenn poundes in

money soe as a conveniente number of them doe attend
and go with my Corpes to Church on the daie of my
funerall Item I do give unto the Companie of Cord-
waynors in London the sume of Fiftie poundes in money
to this end and purpose and upon trust and confidence
that they will laie out or imploye the same in such care-
full and good sorte and manner as that the benefitt
and proffitt which shall come be made or arise of or by
the same and from tyme to tyme for ever maie yerely
and every yeare be given and distributed unto and
amongst such poore ould or decrepitt Sons free of the
said companie as shall att or after every quarter daie
used by the said Company for meetinge together at
their hall come thether for relief and that shall be either
in greate wante distresse and necessitie or stand in
neede of relief the care whereof I doe leave and committ
to the said Companie and their successors to be ordered
and disposed of by them in such good manner as that
some reasonable relief and benefitt thereby maie come
and accrew unto such poore members of the said Companie as I have before expressed and declared yerely
and for ever and att such tymes in the yeare by me intended and lymitted by this my will alsoe I do will that
the some of Tenn poundes in money be given and
delivered by my Executrix to make such and soe maine
of the said Companie as shall accompaine my Corpes
to the Church a Repast or Dinner on the daie of my
funerall Item I doe give unto the poore of Bremingham
where I was borne the some of Twentie and five poundes
in money which some I will shall be paid and delivered

by my Executrix within as conveniente tyme as shee
reasonablie maie after my decease unto my Brother
John Jennens if he be then livinge and if he be then
deade then into the handes of the Churchwardens of
the said parish of Bremingham aforesaid for the tyme
beinge to this intente and purpose and upon this truste
that he or they to whome the said twentie and five
poundes shall be delivered will take care thereof and
see and cause the same to be imployed and disposed for
the benefitt and relief of the said poore from tyme to
tyme or to given and distributed unto and amongst the
said poore where most neede shall be accordinge as he
or they or such to whose handes the said twentie five
poundes shall come or be delivered shall thinke fitt
Item I doe will and give the some of Thirtie poundes of
lawfull English money to be paid and delivered by my
said Executrix within as convenient tyme as shee
reasonablie maie after my decease unto my said
Brother John Jennens if he be then livinge but if he
be then dead then into the handes of the Churchwardens of the said parish of Krenningham aforesaid
for the tyme beinge to this intente and purpose and
upon speciall truste and confidence that he or they to
whome the said Thirty poundes shall be paid or delivered shall and will laie out and dispose of the same
either in purchase of lands or of annuitie or otherwise
as shall be most conveniente to raise and make thereby
what reasonable proffitt and benefitt can or maie be
yerely and from tyme to tyme for ever which benefitt
and proffitt my minde and will is shall be yerely and

from tyme to tyme for ever given and paid unto some godly and painfull Minister of God's holie word that for the tyme beinge shall preach and deliver the word of god within the said Parish Churche of Bremyngham to the congregacon there assembled upon the Sondaies or Saboth daies for instruction and comfort of their soules and this to be an addettem and increase of meanes towardes his paynes and soe to be done and continewed for ever The care whereof I doe leave and committ unto the said John Jennens my Brother soe longe as he shall live and afterwardes unto the Churchwardens and parishioners of the said parish of Bremingham aforesaid from tyme to tyme for the tyme beinge and for ever all the rest and residue of my goodes chattelles leases and other my personall Estate I doe give and leave unto the said Hester my Wife thee payeinge my debtes and pereormeing my legacies accordinge to the true meaninge of this my will and I doe make constitute and appointe my trustie and lovinge brother and frendes Mr Thomas Thomas Garrad and Mr James Bunch and my sonne in lawe Jacob Garrad Overseers of this my will prayeinge them to be assistinge unto my said wife with their best advice and counsell in and concerninge such affaires and buisnesses whereof shee shall desire their helpe and advice as my truste is they will and whereas by reason of my presente weakenes and buisnesses I maie forgett maine of my frendes with some legacies or remembrancs which if I shall not expresse and declare my will and minde concerninge the same before my decease Then I doe committ and leave the care and respecte therein unto the said Hester my Wife desiringe her that she will give and bestowe upon such frendes as I have omitted or not sett downe such reasonable matter and remembrancs as she shall thinke fitt   This is the will concerninge the personall Estate of the said Mr Ambrose Jennens which was read unto published and declared by him the said Ambrose in the presens of us   Test Thos Cruse William Frishe And as towchinge the disposinge of all such Messuages Landes tenem^{ts} and hereditam^{ts} with their apptences beinge Freehould whereof I stand seized or have anie estate of inheritance I doe will give devise and bequeath the same in manner and forme followeinge   (That is to saie)   Item I will give and bequeathe unto the said Hester my wife all that my Messuage or tenem^t with thapptenncs wherein I now dwell called or knowne by the name or signe of the dripping panne or howsoever the same is called or knowne scittuate lyeinge and beinge in Gracechurch Streete in London Together with all roomes Chambers yardes lightes easem^{ts} comodities and apptenncs to the same Messuage or tenemente belonginge or apperteyninge or therewithall now used or occupied & as it is now in the occupation of the said Ambrose Jennens To have and to hold the same and every parte thereof unto the said Hester my Wife for and duringe the terme of her naturall life onlie and noe longer shee keepinge the same in good and tenantable Estate and repaire which my guifte is and shall be in full recompence and satisfaccon unto the said Hester my Wife of and for all such dower and thirdes and

right and title of dower and other demandes as shee
shall have clayme challenge or demaunde of in
to or out of all or any my freehold messuages landes
tenementes and hereditamentes whatsoever which I
have or am seized of and after the decease of the said
Hester my Wife I will give and devise all the said
messuage or tenemente roomes Chambers and other the
premisses thereunto belonginge or therewith used or
occupied as aforesaid with their apptenncs unto the
said Ambrose Jennens my youngest Sonne and to the
heires of his bodie lawfully begotten or to be begotten
and for defaulte of such yssue the same to remayne
unto the said William Jennes my eldest Sonne and to
his heires and assignes for ever Item I doe give will
and bequeath unto my said Sonne William Jennens
All those my two other Messuages or tenem^{ts} with their
apptenncs scittuate lyeing and beinge in Gracechurch
Streete aforesaid wherein M Roberte Wyburd and
Thomas Parker doe now or of late did inhabitt and
dwell and doe lye or neere adioyne unto the said
Messuage or tenemente called the dripping pann
Together with all Roomes Chambers Yardes void
groundes lights easem^{ts} commodities and apptenncs
whatsoever to the same two messuages or tenemts or
either of them belonginge or apperteyninge or with
them or either of them now used occupied or enjoyed
To have and to hould the same two messuages or
tenemts roomes chambers yardes void grounds lights
easements commodities and other the premisses aforesaid with their apptennances above menconed to be

given unto the said William Jennens unto him the said William my Sonne and to the heires of his bodie lawfullie to be begotten and for defaulte of such yssue the same to remayne unto the said Ambrose Jennens my youngest Sonn and to his heires and assignes for ever And my minde will and true meaninge is that the said Hester my Wife shall duringe the minoritie of my said Sonne William Jennens have and receive the rents and proffits of the said two messuages or tenementes and other the premisses with their apptenncs before menconed to be given unto him and thereof to make and give an accompte and recconinge to him when he shall attaine unto and accomplish his full age of Twentie and one yeares togeather with due paymente and satisfaccon unto him of and for all such and soe much rentes and proffitts as in the meantyme shall be had and received by the said Hester his Mother for the same In Wittnes whereof I the said Ambrose Jennins have to this my present Testamente and last Will sett my hand and seale Dated the day and yeares aforesaid—AMBROSE JENNENS—Signed sealed delivered published and declared by the said Ambrose Jennens for his last Will and Testamente in the presens of us— Simeon Fox   Test. Tho. Cruse and William Frith.

"PROBATUM fuit Testamentum suprascriptum apud London coram Magistro Edmondo pope Legum Doctore Surr$^{to.}$ venerabilis viri Dni Henrici Marten Militis legum etiam Doctoris Curie prerogative Cantuariensis Magistri Custodis sive Commissarij legitime constitut Tertio die Mensis

GOPSAL CHURCH.

Junij Anno Dni iuxta cursum et **Compulaconem**
Ecclesie Anglicane Millesimo **sexcentesimo**
vicesimo quinto Juramento Hestere **Jennens**
relicte Dci Defuncti et Executricio in humodi
Testamento nominat Cui Commissa fuit administraco bonorum iurium et Creditorum Dei
Defuncti De bene et fideliter Administrand
eadem ad Sancta Dei evangelia Jurat."

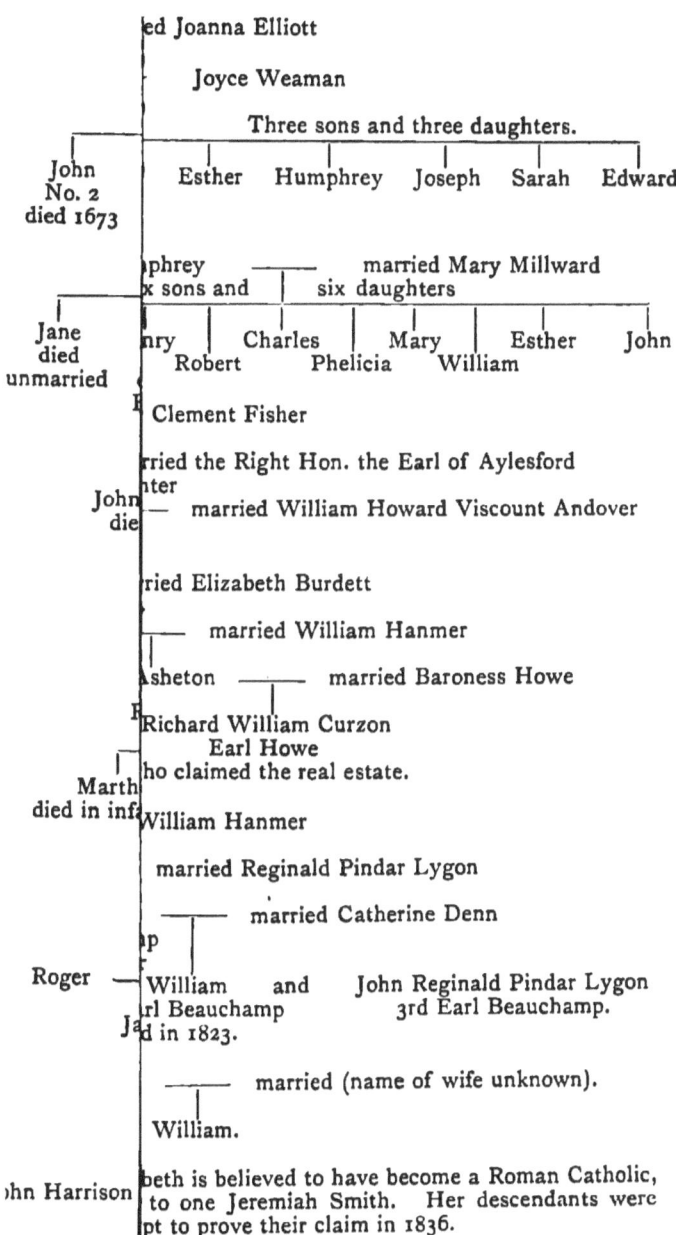

Messrs. Harrison & Willis to the Members of the Jennens Family.

The members of the Jennens Family who take an interest in the affairs of the late William Jennens, deceased, are now so numerous that it becomes impracticable to supply them with written copies of the foregoing Report. It has, therefore, been printed for private circulation, and the same can be obtained on application to Mr. George Willis, 151, Brookhill, Sheffield.

We have to warn our friends against certain over-zealous and unscrupulous persons whose offers of assistance we have declined. We cannot be too careful in accepting proofs. By attempting to prove too much we may jeopardize the case, and a good case, such as we believe ours to be, needs not to be bolstered up by any subtle or unfair contrivance. We solely rely upon the truth. If any of the books or documents which have come into our possession be found to misrepresent anything, they will be rejected as untrue. Even the Family Bible, so long relied upon as evidence of truth, would be laid aside if it could be proved to contain anything false. There are, it is true, certain persons in Birmingham who, doubtless from interested motives, affect to regard the entries therein as forgeries. Others make bolder assertions and say they are. Yet all these persons when challenged as to the proof hesitate and doubt. It was only recently (9th Oct., 1879,) we were requested to destroy the Bible on the ground that it was useless. This we will never do, seeing that it has been verified by four members of the family on oath, and we cannot therefore regard it as untrue. See the joint affidavit of Abraham Ward Rhodes and Mary Ann his wife, and William Rhodes and Eliza his wife, filed 12th March, 1869, paragraph 26.

It will have been observed that the Office Copies of Wills, &c., contain many clerical errors, particularly in the Latin memoranda appended to the Wills, but it was considered best to have them all carefully transcribed.

Finally we request the hearty co-operation of all our kinsmen to enable us to proceed.

CORRECTIONS.

—:o:—

Engraving opposite page 7, for " Moburn Villa " read " Mobourne Mill "

Page 9. Third line from the top, omit " afterwards."

,, 14. Last line but one, for " book " read " register."

,, 16. Third line from the top, for " Nearly all " read " Many of."

,, 78. Seventh line from the bottom, for " returned " read " went."

,, 91.⎫ In the last and first lines, instead of " of Erdington, the
,, 92.⎭ fourth son of Humphrey " read " the son of John No. 2."

,, 107. Third line from the top, for " 82 " read " 182."

www.ingramcontent.com/pod-product-compliance
Lightning Source LLC
Chambersburg PA
CBHW032107220426
43664CB00008B/1164